# Cake Decorating
# with the Kids

# Cake Decorating
## with the Kids

30 modern cakes and bakes for all the family to make

Jill Collins & Natalie Saville

D&C
David and Charles
www.bakeme.com

# Contents

# Let's Decorate!

This book was inspired by our own children, and by the fun we've had making and decorating cakes for the many occasions that suddenly become so important once you have children of your own – school fêtes, end-of-term celebrations, Mother's Day, family get-togethers...

Our children have always been keen to get involved with the baking and cake decorating process, and many a happy afternoon or wet weekend has been spent baking cupcakes, cutting out decorations and swirling with brightly coloured icing before eating messily!

While there are dozens of books written for children that concentrate on developing their baking skills, we couldn't really find any which went that step further, and helped to guide children along the path of true cake decorating – which is, after all, the most exciting part!

We have divided our book into 10 distinct chapters, with one main project and two subsidiary projects each – all of them pretty, quirky or just plain fun. Each chapter has step-by-step instructions for building beautiful themed cakes, with lots of steps that children can do on their own, or with a little help from an adult. At ages 10 through to 14, our own children are pretty much able to do everything, but younger children might need a bit of help with some of the projects. At the end of each project, your children will have created (with a little help from you) a beautiful collection of cakes, cupcakes, whoopie pies or cookies of which they can feel justly proud, and that will garner praise and accolades from all sides (and who doesn't welcome praise after a job well done?). The only thing we can't promise is that you will have any help clearing up the kitchen afterwards – we never quite managed to persuade ours to get involved in that bit!

We have loved creating this book with our children, and hope that you will also enjoy making all the lovely designs with your own children.

Happy decorating!

*Jill & Natalie*

Jake

Joe

Elena

Ashley

# Basic Tools and Equipment

If you enjoy baking and cake decorating, you probably already have all the equipment you need for the projects in this book, and more besides. The lists that follow provide details of everything you need and can be dipped into as part of the basic equipment listed in every project.

## Baking Equipment

- Kitchen scales – accurate weighing of ingredients is essential

- Measuring spoons – for measuring small quantities

- Mixing bowls – for mixing ingredients

- Wooden spoons and spatulas – for mixing and folding

- Electric mixer – makes short work of all your baking but if you don't have one, you can always use a mixing bowl, a wooden spoon and a bit of elbow grease!

- Cake tins (pans)/cupcake tins/baking trays – for baking cakes, cupcakes and cookies

- Greaseproof (wax) paper or re-usable baking parchment – for lining tins (pans) and melting sweets

- Cupcake cases – a variety of styles to suit your projects

- Wire cooling rack – for resting cakes and cookies as they cool

# Cake Decorating Equipment

- Rolling pins – large and small, for rolling out sugarpaste and petal paste

- Small non-stick plastic board – for rolling small amounts of sugarpaste and petal paste

- Plastic dowels – for supporting tiered cakes

- Edible pens – for marking dowels and for quick-and-easy decoration

- Paintbrushes – a variety of different sizes are useful for painting and sticking

- Edible glue – for sticking small pieces of icing together

- Piping (pastry) bags – small for piping royal icing and large for piping buttercream

- Cutters – a variety of shapes and sizes are useful for different projects

- Chocolate moulds – for creating fun and easy chocolate decorations

- Drying mat – a great place to dry small sugarpaste pieces and cut-out shapes

- Piping tubes (tips) – also known as nozzles, a variety of different types and sizes are useful for filling, piping and decorating cakes

- Palette knife – for lifting delicate sugarpaste pieces

- Paste food colourings and edible glitters

- Craft knife – for accurate detailed cutting

- Cocktail sticks (toothpicks) – great for adding tiny amounts of colour

- Sugar shaker – for dredging icing (confectioners') sugar onto your surface to prevent sticking

- Sprinkles – for easy decoration

- Icing smoother – for smoothing cakes that are covered in sugarpaste

# Safety in the Kitchen

Baking and decorating cakes with kids is enormous fun for everyone but of course when working with kids it is always important to make sure that they understand the importance of being safe in the kitchen.

## Rules and Regs

Food safety is a constantly evolving subject, with new rules and regulations being brought in all the time. An example of this is that edible glitter, while non-toxic and completely harmless, has recently been classified as a non-food item, and is therefore not recommended for consumption. We therefore advise removing all glittered objects before eating your cakes.

# Tips to Help Stay Safe

- Wash hands thoroughly with soap and water before starting and often during each decorating session, as it's almost impossible to resist putting little chocolatey fingers in mouths!

- Make sure all surfaces, bowls and utensils are clean and dry.

- Read the whole recipe before you begin – there are often really good tips at the end!

- Keep pets out of the kitchen.

- Tie up long hair and wear an apron to keep clean and avoid transferring germs to food.

- Clean up as you go – an excellent discipline to learn as this avoids accidents caused by spills and prevents foreign bodies finding their way into the food.

- Always ensure an adult uses the oven and handles any hot tins (pans).

- Make sure all cakes and cookies are completely cool before decorating, as icing melts very easily!

- Be vigilant when using knives – sharp knives are often not necessary, other than for carving cakes or cutting around templates, and these aspects are best done by an adult or much older child. For cutting sugarpaste, use old-fashioned flat-bladed bone-handled knives or plastic pointed knives, which are safe for children to use. As a general rule though, children should always be closely supervised when using knives or scissors in the kitchen.

sticky fingers!

lick the spoon – but not until the end!

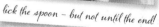

sparkly clean

careful with hot pans

mind your fingers

a job for the grown-ups

# Recipes, Fillings and Toppings

# Recipes

We are firm believers that a cake should taste as good as it looks – and it should look amazing! All these recipes have been meticulously tried and tested and always produce fantastic results if followed carefully, ensuring that you will be absolutely thrilled when you bite into your creations.

## Ingredients

- 275g (9¾oz) unsalted (sweet) butter, softened
- 275g (9¾oz) caster (superfine) sugar
- 5 medium eggs
- 5ml (1 tsp) vanilla extract
- 275g (9¾oz) self-raising (-rising) flour

**Preparation time:** 20 minutes

**Baking time:** 55–60 minutes

**Makes:** 20cm (8in) round cake or 20–24 cupcakes

# Classic Vanilla Sponge Cake

This deliciously light yet moist sponge cake is a must in any baker's repertoire. It is so simple to make and always produces excellent results. It is also very easily adapted to produce other classic flavours (see Flavour Variations).

1 Preheat the oven to 180°C (350°F / Gas 4).

2 Grease and line a 20cm (8in) round tin (pan) with a little softened butter and baking parchment.

3 Cream together the butter and sugar until light and fluffy using an electric whisk or freestanding mixer.

4 Add the eggs one at a time, beating well between each addition. Add the vanilla extract.

5 Sift the flour into the mixture and fold in gently with a large spatula until incorporated.

6 Tip the mixture into your prepared tin (pan) and level the surface with the back of a spoon.

7 Bake for approximately 55 minutes or until a skewer inserted into the centre of the cake comes out clean.

8 Allow to cool in the tin (pan) for 5 minutes before transferring to a wire rack to cool completely.

Alternatively, the same recipe will make perfect cupcakes. Spoon or pipe the mixture into cupcake cases so that they are two-thirds full. Bake for 20–25 minutes (depending on the size of your cupcakes) until the cakes are lightly golden and springy to the touch.

## Flavour Variations

**Chocolate:** for each egg in the recipe, replace 10g (⅜oz) flour with 10g (⅜oz) cocoa powder (unsweetened cocoa)

**Lemon:** replace the vanilla extract with lemon essence

**Orange:** replace the vanilla extract with orange essence

## Ingredients

- 100g (3½oz) unsalted (sweet) butter, softened
- 90g (3oz) soft brown (light brown) sugar
- 1 large (US extra large) egg
- 5ml (1 tsp) vanilla extract
- 80g (2¾oz) maple syrup
- 225g (8oz) self-raising (-rising) flour
- 5ml (1 tsp) bicarbonate of soda (baking soda)
- 5ml (1 tsp) ground cinnamon
- 220g (7¾oz) apple sauce

**Preparation time:** 25 minutes

**Baking time:** 40 minutes

**Makes:** 20cm (8in) round cake or 15–20 cake pops

# Apple and Maple Syrup Cake

This cake is delicious for any occasion but we think it works particularly well as the base for the Apple for the Teacher Cake or the Toffee Apple Cake Pops (see Gifts for Teachers in Projects).

1 Preheat the oven to 180°C (350°F / Gas 4).

2 Grease and line a 20cm (8in) round tin (pan) with a little softened butter and baking parchment.

3 Cream together the butter and sugar until light and fluffy using an electric whisk or freestanding mixer.

4 Add the egg and vanilla and beat well, followed by the maple syrup.

5 Sift together the flour, bicarbonate of soda (baking soda) and cinnamon and stir half into the mixture, folding in gently with a large spatula until incorporated.

6 Fold in half of the apple sauce followed by the remaining flour mixture and the remaining apple sauce.

7 Tip the mixture into your prepared tin (pan) and level the surface with the back of a spoon.

8 Bake for approximately 40 minutes or until a skewer inserted into the centre of the cake comes out clean.

9 Allow to cool in the tin (pan) for 5 minutes before transferring to a wire rack to cool completely.

## Ingredients

- 220g (7¾oz) unsalted (sweet) butter, softened
- 220g (7¾oz) caster (superfine) sugar
- 4 medium eggs
- 3.75ml (¾ tsp) vanilla extract
- 190g (6¾oz) self-raising (-rising) flour
- 30g (1oz) fruity loop-shaped cereal (such as Froot Loops), crushed

Preparation time: 20 minutes
Baking time: 20–25 minutes
Makes: 12 cupcakes

# Cereal Cupcakes

Kids go crazy for these fruity cupcakes – there's just something magical about putting your breakfast cereal into your cupcakes!

**1** Preheat the oven to 180°C (350°F / Gas 4) and line a muffin tin (pan) with cupcake cases.

**2** Cream together the butter and sugar until light and fluffy using an electric whisk or freestanding mixer.

**3** Add the eggs one at a time, beating well between each addition, then add the vanilla extract.

**4** Sift the flour into the mixture along with the crushed cereal. Fold in gently with a large spatula until incorporated.

**5** Spoon or pipe the mixture into the cupcake cases so that they are two-thirds full.

**6** Bake for approximately 20–25 minutes or until the tops spring back when lightly touched.

**7** Allow to cool in the tin (pan) for 5 minutes before transferring to a wire rack to cool completely.

*the perfect size every time*

## Ingredients

- 20cm (8in) round vanilla sponge cake (see Classic Vanilla Sponge Cake)
- 325g (11½oz) vanilla buttercream (see Fillings and Toppings)
- 1 pack white chocolate Candy Melts (400g/14oz)
- 15–30ml (1–2 tbsp) sunflower oil (if needed)

**You will also need:**

- Ice-cream scoop
- Tall thin microwaveable container
- 15–20 lollipop sticks
- Florists' oasis or polystyrene block

Preparation time: 20 minutes

Baking time: 30 minutes

Makes: 15–20 cake pops

# Vanilla Cake Pops

Delicious fluffy cake and soft sweet buttercream, all rolled into a ball and stuck on a stick – what could be more perfect? Cake pops are fun and easy to make, and kids will love getting their hands into the mixture!

1 Removing any crusty edges, crumble the cake in a food processor or by hand, until you have fine crumb-like consistency.

2 Mix in the buttercream (initially with a spoon, but then best done with your hands) until the mixture all comes together smoothly.

3 Use an ice-cream scoop to measure out the mixture and then roll each scoopful into a ball with your hands. Place the balls on a baking tray in the freezer for 15 minutes to harden.

4 Meanwhile, melt the Candy Melts in a tall thin microwaveable container, following the instructions on the packet. Add a couple of spoonfuls of sunflower oil to the melted chocolate to thin it if necessary, and stir.

5 Dip about 1cm (⅜in) of each lollipop stick into the melted chocolate, insert into the cold cake pops and set aside to harden.

6 Leave to rest for around 10 minutes before dipping each cake pop into the chocolate. Try to do this in one fluid motion, ensuring the cake pop is fully covered before removing it from the chocolate. Tap the stick gently on the side of the container to remove any excess chocolate.

7 If decorating with sprinkles, do so immediately otherwise they will not stick properly. If decorating with cut-outs, leave the cake pop to set in an oasis or polystyrene block before securing the decoration with a dab of melted chocolate.

*dip and tap...*

## Flavour Variations

Cake pops are wonderfully versatile and can be made using any combination of cake and buttercream flavours (see Fillings and Toppings). However, be sure to keep the same ratio of cake to buttercream, otherwise your cake pops may be too greasy or may crumble.

**Mint choc:** chocolate sponge cake with peppermint buttercream

**St Clements:** orange sponge cake with lemon buttercream

**Toffee apple:** apple and maple syrup cake with maple syrup icing

*Tip...*
*If your cake pop is too cold when you*
*dip it in the chocolate, it may crack on*
*hardening. If this happens, simply dip it*
*in the chocolate again to cover the crack.*

## Ingredients

- 275g (9¾oz) plain (all-purpose) flour
- 2.5ml (½ tsp) baking powder
- 5ml (1 tsp) bicarbonate of soda (baking soda)
- 115g (4oz) unsalted (sweet) butter, softened
- 200g (7oz) caster (superfine) sugar
- 1 large (US extra large) egg
- 7.5ml (1½ tsp) vanilla extract
- 2.5–5ml (½–1 tsp) paste food colouring in your desired shade (optional)
- 225ml (8fl oz) buttermilk
- 600g (1lb 5oz) vanilla buttercream or other filling of your choice (see Fillings and Toppings)

Preparation time: 20 minutes

Baking time: 10–12 minutes

Makes: 12 whoopie pies

# Vanilla Whoopie Pies

Whoopie pies are the latest craze in the cake world – little mounds of cakey goodness sandwiched together with delicious, gooey fillings. If you manage to resist them long enough to decorate, they are the perfect shape for making the vibrant red ladybirds in the Picnic Party chapter (see Projects).

1 Preheat the oven to 180°C (350°F / Gas 4).

2 Grease two whoopie pie tins (pans) with a little softened butter.

3 Sift together the flour, baking powder and bicarbonate of soda (baking soda) and set aside.

4 In a separate bowl, cream together the butter and sugar until light and fluffy using an electric whisk or freestanding mixer.

5 Add the egg and vanilla and beat until well combined.

6 If colouring your whoopies, add the paste food colouring to the buttermilk and stir well.

7 Fold in half the flour mixture, followed by half the buttermilk. Repeat with the remaining ingredients.

8 Drop a level small ice-cream scoopful of batter into each well of the tins (pans).

9 Bake for approximately 12 minutes or until the whoopies feel just firm to the touch.

10 Allow to cool in the tins (pans) for 5 minutes before transferring to a wire rack to cool completely.

11 Spread or pipe vanilla buttercream (or any other filling of your choice) over one whoopie half and sandwich together with the other half.

*Tip...*

*If you enjoy making whoopie pies, check out our previous book Bake Me I'm Yours... Whoopie Pies for lots more recipes and decorating ideas.*

## Ingredients

- 200g (7oz) unsalted (sweet) butter, softened
- 200g (7oz) caster (superfine) sugar
- 1 medium egg
- 2.5ml (½ tsp) vanilla extract
- 400g (14oz) plain (all-purpose) flour

Preparation time: 20 minutes + 2 hours chilling time

Baking time: 8–12 minutes

Makes: 12–15 large cookies

# Vanilla Sugar Cookies

Baking cookies is a fun (and delicious!) activity to do with the kids, as even the youngest can get involved with the rolling of dough and cutting out of shapes. This recipe can easily be adapted to suit everyone's tastes (see Flavour Variations).

1 Line two baking trays with baking parchment.

2 Using an electric whisk or freestanding mixer, cream together the butter and sugar until light and fluffy (about two minutes). Be careful not to over beat at this stage or the cookies may spread during baking.

3 Beat in the egg and vanilla extract.

4 Sift in the flour and beat with a wooden spoon until the dough just comes together.

5 Tip the dough onto a floured work surface and bring together into a ball, handling it as little as possible at this stage.

6 Wrap in cling film (plastic wrap) and refrigerate for an hour.

7 Roll the dough out evenly on a floured surface to approximately 4mm (⅛in) thick. Cut shapes using cookie cutters and place them on the lined baking trays. Gather up and re-roll the trimmings until all the dough is used up.

8 Refrigerate again for an hour. Halfway through the chilling time, preheat the oven to 180°C (350°F / Gas 4).

9 Bake the cookies for 8–12 minutes (depending on size) until lightly golden. Transfer to a wire rack and allow to cool completely before decorating.

## Flavour Variations

**Chocolate:** replace 70g (2½oz) flour with 70g (2½oz) cocoa powder (unsweetened cocoa)

**Lemon:** replace the vanilla extract with the finely grated zest of 1 lemon

**Cinnamon:** add 5ml (1 tsp) ground cinnamon

# Fillings and Toppings

Every delicious cake needs a delicious filling, and here are some of our favourites. Filling and crumb coating a cake with buttercream or ganache before decorating it adds moistness to the cake and allows it to remain beautifully fresh for three to four days when kept at room temperature (see Filling and Crumb Coating a Cake in Techniques).

## Ingredients

- 250g (8¾oz) unsalted butter, softened
- 500g (1lb 1½oz) icing (confectioners') sugar, sifted
- 5ml (1 tsp) vanilla extract
- 15–30ml (1–2 tbsp) milk (as needed)
- Paste food colouring (optional)

**Preparation time:** 10 minutes

**Makes:** enough to fill and crumb coat a 20cm (8in) round cake, or to spread 24 cupcakes or swirl 15 cupcakes

# Vanilla Buttercream

Vanilla is the most versatile buttercream of all – made extra tasty by adding a layer of raspberry or strawberry jam. It is delicious in its own right, but also invaluable as a base for so many other flavours (see Flavour Variations).

1 Whisk the butter with an electric whisk or freestanding mixer until light and fluffy.

2 Gradually beat in the sifted icing (confectioners') sugar and vanilla, adding milk as needed, until well incorporated and soft.

3 Store in a bowl covered with cling film (plastic wrap) until needed. If making the day before, store in the fridge and bring back to room temperature before using.

## Flavour Variations

For all these alternatives, omit the vanilla extract, and add/substitute the following:

**Chocolate:** replace one-fifth of the icing (confectioners') sugar with the same weight of good-quality cocoa powder (unsweetened cocoa). You may need to add slightly more milk to mix

**Lemon:** add 200g (7oz) good-quality lemon curd to 750g (1lb 10½oz) buttercream and stir in gently. You may want to add slightly less milk at the mixing stage, as the lemon curd will loosen the buttercream

**Peppermint:** replace the vanilla extract with peppermint essence and add a dot or two of green paste food colouring. Add a few chocolate chips and you have mint choc chip!

## Buttercream Tips

- As with all baking, it is important to ensure that your ingredients are at room temperature before you start. If butter or milk is used straight from the fridge they will not blend completely and your buttercream may be flecked with tiny lumps of butter. Not a disaster, but it does spoil the look of the finished cake.

- If you forget to take the milk and butter out of the fridge beforehand, cut the butter into 1cm (⅜in) slices and place on a microwaveable plate, pour the milk into a small microwaveable jug, and heat for around 10–30 seconds each in the microwave.

- For vanilla buttercream, make sure you use good-quality vanilla extract rather than essence, as this gives a much richer flavour.

- Turn your vanilla or lemon buttercream any colour you fancy using paste food colouring – use a cocktail stick (toothpick) to add colour gradually, stirring well between each addition.

- Buttercream freezes well, provided it is kept in an airtight, plastic container. If you want to make a large quantity ahead of a baking session with the kids, freeze it in small batches so you need only defrost the right amount for each cake. Ideally, take the container out the night before and allow the buttercream to reach room temperature naturally, remembering to give it a good stir before use.

## Ingredients

- 40g (1½oz) unsalted (sweet) butter, softened
- 200g (7oz) icing (confectioners') sugar, sifted
- 65ml (4½ tbsp) maple syrup
- 40ml (2½ tbsp) double (heavy) cream

**Preparation time:** 10 minutes

**Makes:** enough to fill and crumb coat a 20cm (8in) round cake, or to spread 24 cupcakes or swirl 15 cupcakes

# Creamy Maple Syrup Icing

Definitely one of our favourite recipes – this icing has to be tasted to be believed!

**1** Whisk the butter with an electric whisk or freestanding mixer until light and fluffy.

**2** Slowly beat in the sifted icing (confectioners') sugar and maple syrup.

**3** Add the cream and whisk on a very low speed, or by hand, to incorporate.

## Ingredients

- 400ml (14fl oz) double (heavy) cream
- 200g (7oz) milk chocolate
- 200g (7oz) dark (semisweet) chocolate (minimum 50 per cent cocoa solids)

**Preparation time:** 10 minutes (plus overnight resting)

**Makes:** enough to fill and crumb coat a 20cm (8in) round cake, or to spread 24 cupcakes or swirl 15 cupcakes

# Chocolate Ganache

Ganache is a very decadent topping, which can be spread on cupcakes or used for filling larger cakes. It tastes best if made with chocolate containing more than 50 per cent cocoa solids, otherwise it tends to have a slightly greasy taste and feel.

1 Pour the cream into a saucepan and gently bring to the boil, stirring regularly to prevent burning. Meanwhile, break the chocolate into squares and place in a large bowl.

2 Once the cream comes to the boil, take off the heat and immediately pour over the chocolate. Allow to sit for a minute, then stir until you have a smooth, glossy mixture. Set aside to cool and thicken overnight.

## Flavour Variations

**Chocolate orange:** replace the milk chocolate with orange-flavoured chocolate

**Chocolate mint:** add 5ml (1 tsp) peppermint essence to the warm ganache

**Chilli chocolate:** for a grown-up kick, replace the dark (semisweet) chocolate with dark (semisweet) chocolate flavoured with chilli

### Tip...
*If you haven't been able to make your ganache the night before, you can speed up the process by placing it in a bowl in the fridge for a few hours, stirring regularly. You can also freeze it ahead of a baking session, bringing it back to room temperature before use.*

# Sugarpaste

Also known as rolled fondant icing, this is widely available in major supermarkets and online. Sugarpaste is easy to roll and colour using paste food colourings (see Colouring Sugarpaste and Petal Paste in Techniques) and is perfect as a base for many of the designs in this book. We don't recommend even trying to make your own – it's a step too far – especially when all the kids want to do is get on with the exciting stuff!

# Petal Paste

Also called modelling paste or flower paste, this is similar to sugarpaste but hardens quicker and can be rolled much more thinly without breaking. It dries to a hard, china-like finish and is perfect for making more delicate items such as flowers and butterflies. For best results, roll out on a non-stick plastic board with a small non-stick rolling pin. For perfect cut outs, the paste needs to be as thin as possible – almost transparent. White petal paste can be coloured in the same way as sugarpaste, though it is available in many different colours from specialist sugarcraft shops and online.

## Ingredients

- 45ml (3 tbsp) cool water
- 18ml (3 heaped tsp) powdered egg white (such as Meri-White)
- 250–300g (8¾–10½oz) icing (confectioners') sugar, sifted

**Preparation time:** 10 minutes

**Makes:** 90ml (6 tbsp) royal icing

# Royal Icing

Royal icing is widely used for piping and sticking. The icing is traditionally made with raw egg white, but we prefer to make ours using powdered egg white (such as Meri-White), which is available from sugarcraft suppliers and online. This means there are no leftover egg yolks and also eliminates any food safety issues, making it suitable for consumption by young children and pregnant women. Royal icing is also readily available as a packet mix from many supermarkets.

*Tip...*

*When beating royal icing by hand, place the bowl on a folded tea towel (dish towel) to avoid slipping.*

**1** Add the water to a large, clean bowl, then sprinkle the powdered egg white on top. Mix vigorously with a wooden spoon until full of bubbles and all the egg white powder has been incorporated.

**2** Add the sifted icing (confectioners') sugar a couple of spoonfuls at a time, beating well with your wooden spoon between each addition, until the icing falls into soft peaks when lifted from the bowl with your spoon.

**3** Transfer the icing immediately to an airtight plastic container, lay some cling film (plastic wrap) directly on top to prevent crusting, then replace the lid and store in the fridge. It will keep for up to two weeks like this. Bring back to room temperature and beat briefly with a wooden spoon or a flat knife before use.

*Tip...*

*If you find your royal icing is too stiff to pipe, put it back into a bowl, add a few drops of water and re-beat. Conversely, if the icing spreads when piped, add more sifted icing (confectioners') sugar a little at a time and re-beat.*

# Quantity Adjustments

All the recipes in this book can be easily adapted to produce the size of cake you require. Baking times may vary depending on your oven, so towards the end of the cooking time, keep an eye on the cake and remove from the oven when it feels springy to the touch and is just beginning to come away from the sides of the tin (pan).

# Sponge Cake

| Cake size/ shape | 15cm (6in) round | 18cm (7in) round / 15cm (6in) square | 20cm (8in) round / 18cm (7in) square | 23cm (9in) round / 20cm (8in) square | 25cm (10in) round / 23cm (9in) square | 28cm (11in) round / 25cm (10in) square | 30cm (12in) round | 30cm (12in) square | Cupcakes (makes 12) |
|---|---|---|---|---|---|---|---|---|---|
| Caster (superfine) sugar | 165g (6oz) | 220g (7³⁄₄oz) | 275g (9³⁄₄oz) | 330g (11½oz) | 440g (15½oz) | 550g (1lb 3½oz) | 660g (1lb 7¼oz) | 770g (1lb 11oz) | 165g (6oz) |
| Unsalted (sweet) butter | 165g (6oz) | 220g (7³⁄₄oz) | 275g (9³⁄₄oz) | 330g (11½oz) | 440g (15½oz) | 550g (1lb 3½oz) | 660g (1lb 7¼oz) | 770g (1lb 11oz) | 165g (6oz) |
| Medium eggs | 3 | 4 | 5 | 6 | 8 | 10 | 12 | 14 | 3 |
| Self-raising (-rising) flour | 165g (6oz) | 220g (7³⁄₄oz) | 275g (9³⁄₄oz) | 330g (11½oz) | 440g (15½oz) | 550g (1lb 3½oz) | 660g (1lb 7¼oz) | 770g (1lb 11oz) | 165g (6oz) |
| Vanilla/lemon essence | 2.5ml (½ tsp) | 5ml (1 tsp) | 5ml (1 tsp) | 5ml (1 tsp) | 10ml (2 tsp) | 10ml (2 tsp) | 10ml (2 tsp) | 15ml (3 tsp) | 2.5ml (½ tsp) |
| Approx baking time | 45 mins | 45–50 mins | 50 mins | 55 mins | 55–60 mins | 1hr 15 mins | 1hr 15 mins | 1hr 30 mins | 22 mins |

# Buttercream

These are the quantities needed to fill and crumb coat different sizes and shapes of cake.

| Cake size/ shape | 15cm (6in) round | 18cm (7in) round / 15cm (6in) square | 20cm (8in) round / 18cm (7in) square | 23cm (9in) round / 20cm (8in) square | 25cm (10in) round / 23cm (9in) square | 28cm (11in) round / 25cm (10in) square | 30cm (12in) round | 30cm (12in) square | Cupcakes (12 iced flat) | Cupcakes (12 swirled) |
|---|---|---|---|---|---|---|---|---|---|---|
| Unsalted (sweet) butter | 175g (6oz) | 200g (7oz) | 250g (8¾oz) | 350g (12¼oz) | 500g (1lb 1½oz) | 550g (1lb 4oz) | 600g (1lb 5oz) | 650g (1lb 7oz) | 125g (4½oz) | 250g (8¾oz) |
| Icing (confectioners') sugar | 350g (12¼oz) | 400g (14oz) | 500g (1lb 1½oz) | 700g (1lb 8½oz) | 1kg (2lb 3¼oz) | 1.1kg (2lb 8oz) | 1.2kg (2lb 10¼oz) | 1.3kg (2lb 14oz) | 250g (8¾oz) | 500g (1lb 1½oz) |
| Vanilla extract | 2.5ml (½ tsp) | 3.75ml (¾ tsp) | 5ml (1 tsp) | 7.5ml (1½ tsp) | 10ml (2 tsp) | 10ml (2 tsp) | 11.25ml (2¼ tsp) | 12.5ml (2½tsp) | 2.5ml (½ tsp) | 5ml (1 tsp) |

# Sugarpaste

The following table gives a guide to the quantities of sugarpaste needed to cover cakes and boards. There may be a little sugarpaste left over, but having a slightly larger quantity makes it much easier to roll and cover both cakes and boards. Wrap any leftovers tightly in cling film (plastic wrap) and store in a plastic bag.

| Shape/size | Item | 15cm (6in) | 20cm (8in) | 25cm (10in) | 30cm (12in) | 35cm (14in) |
|---|---|---|---|---|---|---|
| Round | Cake | 800g (1lb 12¼oz) | 1.25kg (2lb 12oz) | 1.5kg (3lb 5oz) | 2.25kg (5lb) | |
| | Board | 250g (8¾oz) | 600g (1lb 5oz) | 850g (1lb 14oz) | 1kg (2lb 3¼oz) | 1.2kg (2lb 10¼oz) |
| Square | Cake | 1kg (2lb 3¼oz) | 1.5kg (3lb 5oz) | 1.75kg (3lb 13¾oz) | 2.5kg (5lb 8oz) | |
| | Board | 350g (12¼oz) | 700g (1lb 8½oz) | 900g (2lb) | 1.25kg (2lb 12oz) | 1.5kg (3lb 5oz) |

# Projects

# Family Celebration

Family gatherings are a great excuse to indulge your passion for cake decorating – and being family, they're always going to be impressed with your efforts! This dramatic three-tier celebration cake will leave them speechless with admiration – no need to tell anybody how easy it is to make!

## Materials

- 15cm (6in) square filled cake
- 20cm (8in) square filled cake covered with white sugarpaste
- 25cm (10in) square filled cake covered with blue sugarpaste
- 35cm (14in) square cake drum covered with white sugarpaste and edged with black ribbon
- Sugarpaste: 1kg (2¼lb) white, 100g (3½oz) black
- Petal paste: 10g (⅜oz) blue, 20g (¾oz) white, 20g (¾oz) black
- 75ml (5 tbsp) royal icing
- Icing (confectioners') sugar for dusting
- Edible glue
- Edible glitter: white and black

## Equipment

- 5 plastic dowels
- Star shaped cutters – small, medium and large
- 5 lengths of white florists' wire, cut in half and hooked at one end
- Ribbon: 168cm (66in) black; 84cm (33in) white
- Piping (pastry) bag with a no.2 tube (tip)
- White posy pick (approx 1.5cm/½in diameter)
- Basic equipment (see Basic Tools and Equipment)

*moisten the stars with a damp paintbrush*

### Jobs that can be done in advance:

☆ **Cover the cake board** (see Filling and Covering in Techniques)

☆ **Colour the pastes**

☆ **Cut, glitter and wire the stars** (see Steps 6–7)

### Great jobs for the kids:

❂ **Make the zebra stripes** (see Step 1)

❂ **Make the stars** (see Step 6)

❂ **Pipe the dots** (see Step 8)

*pour unused glitter back into its pot*

# Stunning Starburst Cake

1 Roll out the black sugarpaste to an even 2mm (1/16in) thickness and cut thin pointed strips of varying lengths to make the zebra stripes.

2 Wash your hands, the rolling pin and the surface thoroughly to remove all traces of black. Ensure there is plenty of icing (confectioners') sugar on your surface and roll out the white sugarpaste to an even 4mm (1/8in) thickness to approximately 30cm (12in) square.

*Tip...*

*It's crucial to ensure there's lots of icing (confectioners') sugar under the white sugarpaste before laying on the black strips, as if it sticks to the surface the entire thing will be wasted and you'll have to start again.*

3 Place the black strips on top of the white paste in a random pattern, radiating out from the centre. Roll your rolling pin once or twice in both directions over the pattern to incorporate the black paste into the white.

4 Use the zebra-striped paste to cover the 15cm (6in) cake in the usual way (see Filling and Covering in Techniques) and discard the trimmings, all but a small ball of white sugarpaste for the posy pick.

**5** Spread 15ml (1 tbsp) royal icing in the centre of the covered cake board and position the 25cm (10in) cake squarely on top. Dowel this cake with the plastic dowels (see Dowelling in Techniques). Spread another 15ml (1 tbsp) royal icing in the centre of this cake on top of the dowels, and then carefully drop the 20cm (8in) cake on top, again taking care to position it centrally. Repeat for the 15cm (6in) cake and edge all three cakes with ribbon using white for the middle tier and black for the top and bottom tiers (see Trimming a Cake and Board with Ribbon in Techniques).

**6** Roll out the black and white petal pastes very thinly, cut four large stars from each colour and set aside. From the remaining pastes, cut four medium and two small white stars, two medium and four small black stars and four small blue stars.

**7** Lay the stars out in coloured pairs and sandwich each pair together on the end of a wire with a dab of edible glue. Moisten all the white stars with a damp paintbrush (including the large ones that were set aside) and sprinkle with edible white glitter, not forgetting to glitter both sides of the wired stars. Repeat with the black glitter for the black stars.

**8** Using a dab of edible glue, randomly stick the large stars on the bottom tier of the cake. Place the remaining royal icing into a piping (pastry) bag with a no.2 tube (tip) and pipe white dots in a regular pattern around the middle tier of the cake (see Piping and Flooding in Techniques).

**9** Fill the posy pick with a small ball of white sugarpaste to anchor the wires then push the pick into the centre of the cake until it is level with the surface. Arrange the wires in the posy pick by cutting to varying lengths and pushing firmly into the sugarpaste.

**10** Pipe a large dot of royal icing over the top of the pick if needed, to neaten.

*Tip...*
*Make sure you shake off excess glitter well or it may transfer to the cake and spoil the clean look.*

## Materials

- 15 cake pops on sticks
- 1 pack white chocolate Candy Melts (400g/14oz)
- Sanding sugar: 1 jar white, 1 jar blue
- 10g (3/8oz) blue petal paste
- Blue edible glitter

## Equipment

- Tall thin microwavable container
- Florists' oasis or polystyrene block
- Large star cutter
- Red ribbon
- Basic equipment (see Basic Tools and Equipment)

*Tip...*
*Use the same star cutter as used on your celebration cake for a lovely co-ordinated look.*

*Jobs that can be done in advance:*

☆ Make the cake pops (see Vanilla Cake Pops in Recipes)

☆ Cut and glitter the stars (see Step 4)

*Great jobs for the kids:*

✪ So easy they can do it all!

*Tip...*
*For a fun display, present your cake pops in a vase filled with sweets.*

# Let's Celebrate Cake Pops

Decorating these cake pops simply, using cut-out shapes and sanding sugar, means that these little delicacies are easy enough for even the youngest of children to make.

1 Melt the Candy Melts in a tall thin microwaveable container, following the instructions on the packet.

2 Dip a cake pop into the chocolate and tap the stick gently on the side of the container to remove any excess chocolate. Immediately pour white sanding sugar all over the cake pop, twisting it to ensure complete coverage. Place a saucer underneath to collect the excess sugar for re-use.

3 Push the cake pop into the oasis or polystyrene and leave to set. Repeat the process for four more cake pops then use blue sanding sugar for another five.

4 Roll out the petal paste to an even 2mm (1/16in) thickness and cut out five stars. Moisten with a damp paintbrush and sprinkle with blue edible glitter. Dip the remaining cake pops in the chocolate and once set, decorate each one with a star, fixing it in place with a dot of melted chocolate.

5 Tie ribbon bows around each stick.

## Materials

- 18 balloon-shaped cookies
- Royal icing: 15ml (1 tbsp) each white, red, blue
- Flooding icing: 45ml (3 tbsp) each white, red, blue (see Piping and Flooding in Techniques)
- A few lengths of liquorice (approx 20cm/8in each)

## Equipment

- Balloon-shaped cookie cutter
- 3 piping (pastry) bags with no.2 tubes (tips)
- 3 piping (pastry) bags without tubes (tips)
- Basic equipment (see Basic Tools and Equipment)

# Party Balloon Cookies

These balloon-shaped cookies complement the celebration cake beautifully and can be iced in any colour to match the theme of your party.

1 As your cookies come out of the oven, use a skewer to push a hole into the bottom of each balloon to hold the strings.

2 When completely cool, outline and flood the cookies in matching colours using royal icing in a piping (pastry) bag with a no.2 tube (tip) for the outlines, and flooding icing in a bag without a tube (tip) for flooding (see Piping and Flooding in Techniques). Allow to dry completely (preferably overnight).

3 To finish, secure the liquorice strings into the balloons with a dab of royal icing.

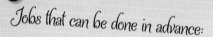

### Jobs that can be done in advance:

☆ Bake the cookies (see Vanilla Sugar Cookies in Recipes)

### Great jobs for the kids:

✪ Cut the balloon shapes from the cookie dough (see Vanilla Sugar Cookies in Recipes)
✪ Flood the balloons with royal icing (see Piping and Flooding in Techniques)

*flooding cookies takes concentration*

# White Christmas

This incredibly stylish and elegant Christmas cake will make a stunning centrepiece for your Christmas table and is made all the more special by the fact that it can be decorated by the children – the perfect family bonding activity in the run up to Christmas.

## Materials

- 25cm (10in) round filled cake, covered with white sugarpaste and trimmed with ice-blue ribbon
- 35cm (14in) round cake drum covered with ice-blue sugarpaste and edged with silver ribbon
- 75ml (5 tbsp) royal icing
- 20 clear mints
- Readymade sugardough: 180g (6⅜oz) white
- Edible ink pens: black, orange
- Paste food colouring: brown, red
- White edible glitter

## Equipment

- Small scissors
- Star cutters: various sizes
- Piping (pastry) bag with a no.2 tube (tip)
- Basic equipment (see Basic Tools and Equipment)

*ahhh... so lovely!*

### Jobs that can be done in advance:

☆ Cover the cake and board (see Filling and Covering in Techniques)
☆ Make the lake (see Step 2)
☆ Make the swans (see Step 3)
☆ Make the trees (see Step 4)

### Great jobs for the kids:

✪ Make the swans (see Step 3)
✪ Cut out and assemble the trees (see Step 4)
✪ Pipe dots on the cake (see Step 6)
✪ Make the robin (see Step 7)

*you do it like this...*

# Winter Wonderland Cake

1 Spread 15ml (1 tbsp) royal icing in the centre of the covered cake board and position the cake on top.

2 **For the lake** Preheat the oven to 180°C (350°F / Gas 4). Lay out the mints, touching each other, in an oval pattern in the centre of a baking tray lined with a sheet of re-usable baking parchment. Place in the oven for 5–10 minutes or until completely melted. Remove from the oven and allow to cool on the tray.

3 **For the swans** Use 30g (1oz) white sugardough to form two teardrop shapes. With the end of a small pair of scissors snip 'feathers' into the bodies and allow to dry. Use 6g (¼oz) of the sugardough to shape two necks, and 24g (⅞oz) to cut out four wings. Use the snipping technique to make feathers on the wings and attach to the bodies with a dab of royal icing. When the necks are dry, draw eyes and beaks with edible ink pens and secure to the bodies with royal icing.

*Tip...*
*Attach the wings to the bodies before they dry so that you can mould them into shape.*

**4** **For the trees** Roll out 120g (4¼oz) white sugardough to a 3mm (⅛in) thickness. Cut out approximately 30 stars of varying sizes and set aside to dry. Place the stars on top of each other, in size order, starting with the largest first. Secure each star to the next with a dab of royal icing and twist each star slightly to offset the points. Use approximately 18 stars to make the large tree and 12 stars to make the small tree. Top the trees with a small cone of sugardough, fixed with a dot of royal icing and leave to dry.

**5** Peel the cooled mint from the parchment and position on the cake. Roughly spread royal icing all around the edge of the lake to secure and disguise the edge. Fix the swans on the lake and the trees to the cake with royal icing. Sprinkle white edible glitter over the trees.

*Tip...*
*Try not to touch the melted mints too much as fingerprints show up!*

**6** Pipe dots in a symmetrical pattern around the edge of the cake using a piping (pastry) bag with a no.2 tube (tip) (see Piping and Flooding in Techniques).

**7** **For the robin** Colour a small piece of leftover sugardough with brown paste food colouring and roll into a small semi-circle approximately 3cm (1¼in) wide. Holding the semi-circle between your thumbs and forefingers and the curved side at the bottom, pinch out one side to form the tail and make a tiny pinch at the other end for the beak and mould to shape. Colour a tiny piece of leftover sugardough with red paste food colouring and stick to the breast with the tiniest dot of water. Use the black edible ink pen to mark the eyes. Secure the robin to a tree with a dab of royal icing.

*Tip...*
*Make sure the swans' necks are really dry before drawing on the beaks and eyes, otherwise the pen may make indents in the heads.*

## Materials

- 12 star-shaped cookies in increasing sizes
- Small edible silver balls
- 30–45ml (2–3 tbsp) white fondant icing (from a packet mix)

## Equipment

- Star cutters: various sizes
- Basic equipment (see Basic Tools and Equipment)

**Jobs that can be done in advance:**

☆ Bake the cookies (see Vanilla Sugar Cookies in Recipes)

**Great jobs for the kids:**

✪ So easy they can do it all!

# Christmas Cookie Tree

A great project for the little ones – this cookie tree makes a fantastic addition to your festive table.

1 Make the fondant icing following the instructions on the packet. Mix well until you have an easily spreadable consistency. (Alternatively use flooding icing – see Piping and Flooding in Techniques.)

2 Using a teaspoon, spread the fondant icing all over the top of each cookie and stick an edible silver ball onto each point. Don't worry if the icing dribbles down the side – it just makes it look more like snow!

3 Set the cookies aside to dry for a couple of hours then assemble the tree, starting with the largest cookie, fixing each star to the one below with a dab of fondant icing and twisting each star slightly to offset the points.

*Tip...*
*If you prefer, you can push the silver balls into the cookie dough before baking, which is less fiddly than sticking them on afterwards.*

*excellent spreading boys!*

## Materials

- Half quantity chocolate ganache, chilled for at least 12 hours
- 30ml (2 tbsp) cocoa powder (unsweetened cocoa)
- Sugarpaste: 40g (1½oz) white, 20g (¾oz) green, 15g (½oz) red
- 15ml (1 tbsp) icing (confectioners') sugar

## Equipment

- 24 brown petit four cases
- Cutters: mini holly leaf and small flower
- Cocktail stick (toothpick)
- Basic equipment (see Basic Tools and Equipment)

### Jobs that can be done in advance:

☆ Make the chocolate ganache (see Fillings and Toppings)

### Great jobs for the kids:

✪ So easy they can do it all!

# Festive Truffle Puddings

This is definitely one that the kids are going to love. But beware... they WILL get covered in chocolate!

1 Sieve the cocoa powder (unsweetened cocoa) onto a flat plate.

2 Scoop a teaspoonful of the set ganache (approximately 15g/1½oz) and roll gently into a ball between the palms of your hands, taking care not to handle too much at this stage as it can easily melt.

3 Roll the truffle in cocoa to cover it completely then drop into a petit four case and set aside. Repeat to make 24 truffles in total.

4 Roll out the white sugarpaste to a 1mm (⅟₁₆in) thickness and cut out 24 small flowers. Mix the icing (confectioners') sugar with a few drops of water to make a thick glue and use this to stick one flower on top of each truffle (a cocktail stick/toothpick is useful for this job).

5 Roll out the green sugarpaste to a 1–2mm (⅟₁₆in) thickness and cut out 72 mini holly leaves. Roll 72 tiny balls from the red sugarpaste and attach three leaves and three berries on top of each truffle using the sugar glue. Store in a cool place for up to three days.

### Tip...
Separate all the petit four cases before starting, as once you get going your fingers get very chocolatey!

*don't squish too hard!*

# Easter Sunday

Sometimes Easter can be just too chocolatey and it's nice to have a lighter, fresher alternative. This fabulous chick cake looks so impressive but is actually incredibly easy to create. Arm yourself with a large piping (pastry) bag filled with yellow buttercream and you're halfway there!

## Materials

- 18cm (7in) and 23cm (9in) round filled cakes
- 52cm (20in) square cake drum covered with green sugarpaste and edged with orange ribbon
- Petal paste: 16g (½oz) orange, 30g (1oz) white, 5g (¼oz) black
- Royal icing: 30ml (2 tbsp) white, 15ml (1 tbsp) orange
- 2kg (4lb 6½oz) lemon or vanilla buttercream, coloured yellow
- Edible glue
- 8 twig-shaped snacks (such as Twiglets)

## Equipment

- Daisy cutters: medium and small
- Oval cutters: large and medium
- Paintbrush
- Large piping (pastry) bag with a large star tube (tip)
- Small piping (pastry) bag with a no.2 tube (tip)
- Basic equipment (see Basic Tools and Equipment)

*spring is here!*

### Jobs that can be done in advance:

☆ Cover the board (see Filling and Covering in Techniques)
☆ Make the flowers (see Step 2)
☆ Make the chick's features (see Steps 1–3)

### Great jobs for the kids:

✪ Make the flowers (see Step 2)
✪ Make the chick's features (see Steps 1–3)
✪ Pipe the chick – it doesn't matter if its feathers are a bit ruffled! (see Step 5)

*round and round we go...*

# Fluffy Chick Cake

1 Roll out the orange petal paste to a 1mm (¹⁄₁₆in) thickness and cut out a medium daisy for the flower on the chick's head. Divide the remaining paste in half and shape each part into a concave triangle for the beak.

2 Roll out the white petal paste to a 1mm (¹⁄₁₆in) thickness and cut out two large ovals, seven medium daisies and 14 small daisies. Also roll two tiny balls for the sparkle in the eyes and one larger ball for the centre of the orange flower.

3 Roll out the black petal paste to a 1mm (¹⁄₁₆in) thickness and cut out two medium ovals for the eyes and six thin strips approximately 4cm (1½in) long for the eyelashes. Stick the black ovals onto the white ovals with a dab of edible glue and add the tiny white balls for the sparkle. Bend each eyelash into a curved shape and set aside to dry along with all the other features and flowers.

*Tip...*
*Don't be tempted to overfill your piping (pastry) bag with buttercream as it tends to ooze out the top and make a mess.*

4 Meanwhile, spread 15ml (1 tbsp) white royal icing towards the top of the covered cake board and position the 18cm (7in) cake for the head. Repeat with the 23cm (9in) cake for the body, ensuring that the cakes are touching and centred on the board.

5 Fill a large piping (pastry) bag fitted with a large star tube (tip) with around a third of the buttercream and pipe stars all over the cakes, starting on the outside and working in (see Piping and Flooding in Techniques). Refill your piping bag with buttercream as necessary until the cakes are completely covered.

6 While the buttercream is still soft, position the twig-shaped snacks against the bottom of the larger cake for the feet. Push the beak into the buttercream just below the centre of the smaller cake, ensuring it remains slightly open. Position the eyes on the cake and place the eyelashes sweeping to the side of each eye. Place the orange flower on top of the chick's head and stick the remaining white ball in the centre.

7 Scatter the daisies randomly around the bottom of the board, fixing with a dab of royal icing. Using a small piping (pastry) bag with a no.2 tube (tip) pipe a dot of orange royal icing in the centre of each flower.

*Tip...*
*When piping the sides of the cake, start at the bottom to give the rows of stars above some support.*

## Materials

- 12 cupcakes baked in green cupcake cases
- 375g (13¼oz) buttercream, coloured green
- Sugarpaste: 200g (7oz) yellow, 20g (¾oz) white, 5g (¼oz) orange, 5g (¼oz) black
- Edible glue

## Equipment

- Large piping (pastry) bag with a star tube (tip)
- Assorted small daisy cutters
- Basic equipment (see Basic Tools and Equipment)

### Jobs that can be done in advance:

☆ Bake the cupcakes (see Classic Vanilla Sponge Cake in Recipes)
☆ Colour the buttercream

### Great jobs for the kids:

✪ So easy they can do it all!

*draw eyes with edible pen if you like*

# Baby Chick Cupcakes

These cute little cupcakes are as fun to make as they are to eat – mini versions of the Fluffy Chick Cake!

1 Roll out the white sugarpaste to a 2mm (1/16in) thickness and cut out 24 assorted daisies. Roll tiny balls of yellow sugarpaste and stick in the centre of each daisy with a dab of edible glue.

2 For each chick, roll 10g (⅜oz) yellow sugarpaste into a ball for the body and 5g (¼oz) for the head. Fix the head on the body with edible glue. Use tiny balls of black sugarpaste for the eyes and orange for the beaks, securing both with edible glue.

3 Using a large piping (pastry) bag with a star tube (tip), pipe green buttercream stars all over the tops of your cupcakes and place your chicks and flowers on top before the buttercream sets.

### Tip...
*To make the buttercream look like grass, pull the tube (tip) away sharply after you pipe each star.*

## Materials

- 12–15 (depending on the size of your cutters) egg-shaped cookies
- Sugarpaste: 200g (7oz) white, 200g (7oz) yellow
- Petal paste: 20g (¾oz) white, 20g (¾oz) yellow
- Royal icing: 15ml (1 tbsp) white, 15ml (1 tbsp) yellow

## Equipment

- Daisy cutters: medium and small
- Paint palettes
- Egg-shaped cookie cutter
- 2 piping (pastry) bags with no.2 tubes (tips)
- Small paintbrush
- Basic equipment (see Basic Tools and Equipment)

### Jobs that can be done in advance:

☆ Bake the cookies (see Vanilla Sugar Cookies in Recipes)

☆ Make the daisies (see Step 1)

### Great jobs for the kids:

✿ So easy they can do it all!

# Easter Egg Cookies

These sunny, cheerful little cookies are easy enough for even the youngest of children to decorate.

**1** Roll out the white and yellow petal pastes to a 1mm (¹⁄₁₆in) thickness and cut out a selection of small and medium daisies. Dry the medium-sized daisies for a couple of hours in paint palettes so that they take on a cupped shape.

**2** Roll out the white and yellow sugarpastes to a 2mm (¹⁄₁₆in) thickness and cut out egg shapes using the same cutter that was used to cut the cookies. Brush the cookies sparingly with water and place the sugarpaste ovals on top.

**3** Decorate the cookies with the daisies, securing each with a dot of royal icing and pipe dots in the daisy centres in contrasting colours.

### Tip...
Turn these into chocolate Easter eggs by baking chocolate cookies and decorating with sprinkles and tiny sweets.

*utter concentration*

# Happy Halloween

Ring the changes for your trick-or-treaters this year and display this BOOtiful Halloween cake in your window instead of the usual pumpkin lantern – no messy carving involved, much tastier to eat afterwards and far healthier than all that candy – better for your teeth too!

## Materials

- 15cm (6in) and 20cm (8in) round filled cakes, covered with violet sugarpaste
- 30cm (12in) round cake drum covered with grey sugarpaste and edged with black ribbon
- Royal icing: 45ml (3 tbsp) white, 15ml (1 tbsp) black
- Petal paste: 80g (2⁷⁄₈oz) white, 20g (³⁄₄oz) orange
- Sugarpaste: 150g (5¼oz) white, 120g (4¼oz) black, 100g (3½oz) grey, 10g (³⁄₈oz) yellow
- Edible glitter: white hologram and yellow
- Edible glue

## Equipment

- 5 plastic dowels
- Silver ribbon, approximately 80cm (30in) long
- Round cutters: 5mm (¹⁄₈in), 1cm (³⁄₈in), 2cm (³⁄₄in), 5.5cm (2¹⁄₈in)
- Templates: ghosts and house (see Templates)
- Paintbrush
- 2 piping (pastry) bags with no.2 tubes (tips)
- Basic equipment (see Basic Tools and Equipment)

*eat it if you dare!*

### Jobs that can be done in advance:

- ☆ Cover the board (see Filling and Covering in Techniques)
- ☆ Colour the pastes
- ☆ Make the ghosts, moon, haunted houses, pebbles and cats (see Steps 2–6)

### Great jobs for the kids:

- ✪ Assemble the haunted houses (see Step 3)
- ✪ Make the pebbles, cats, clouds and spider (see Steps 5–8)

*mind your fingers*

# Haunted House Cake

1 Spread 15ml (1 tbsp) white royal icing in the centre of the covered cake board, position the 20cm (8in) cake centrally on top and dowel the cake (see Dowelling in Techniques). Spread another 15ml (1 tbsp) white royal icing in the centre of the 20cm (8in) cake on top of the dowels then carefully drop the 15cm (6in) cake on top, again taking care to position it centrally. Trim the top tier with silver ribbon (see Trimming a Cake and Board with Ribbon in Techniques).

2 **For the ghosts and moon** Roll out the white petal paste to a 1mm (¹⁄₁₆in) thickness and cut out two large and three small ghosts using the templates. Use the 5mm (¹⁄₈in) round cutter to cut two eyes and a mouth from each large ghost. From the trimmings, use the 5.5cm (2¹⁄₈in) round cutter to cut out a moon. Set all aside to dry completely then moisten with a damp paintbrush and sprinkle with white edible glitter.

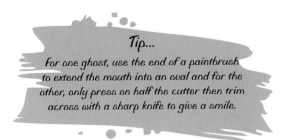

*Tip...*
*For one ghost, use the end of a paintbrush to extend the mouth into an oval and for the other, only press on half the cutter then trim across with a sharp knife to give a smile.*

3 **For each haunted house (four in total)** Roll out the orange petal paste to a 1mm (¹⁄₁₆in) thickness and cut out a house using the template. Roll out the yellow sugarpaste and 5g (¼oz) of the black sugarpaste to a 1mm (¹⁄₁₆in) thickness and cut three yellow windows and a black door as shown on the template. Moisten the windows with a damp paintbrush and sprinkle with yellow edible glitter. Secure the windows and doors to the houses with edible glue. Stick the houses randomly around the cakes using edible glue.

4 **For each tree (two in total)** Roll 30g (1oz) black sugarpaste into three thin sausage shapes, each 20cm (8in) long. Twist the bottoms together for 6cm (2³⁄₈in), leaving the ends clear for the roots. Attach the trunk to the base of the cake then spread the branches around the sides, securing with edible glue. Use another 10g (³⁄₈oz) black sugarpaste to make extra branches to fill out the tree. Position the second tree at the back of the cake.

5 **For the pebbles** Knead the grey sugarpaste with 10g (³⁄₈oz) white to produce a marbled effect. Roll into pebbles and fix around the base of the bottom tier with a little royal icing, leaving gaps around the houses and trees.

6 **For each cat (two in total)** Roll out 10g (³⁄₈oz) black sugarpaste to a 2mm (¹⁄₁₆in) thickness and cut out a 5.5cm (2¹⁄₈in) circle. Reposition the cutter 1cm (³⁄₈in) down from the top of the circle and re-cut, leaving a semi-circular body. Cut a 2cm (¾in) circle for the head use trimmings to make ears and a tail. Attach randomly to the cake with edible glue.

7 **For the clouds** Mould the white sugarpaste into two cloud shapes. Moisten, sprinkle with white edible glitter and fix to the top of the cake with a dab of royal icing. Cut a 1–2cm (³⁄₈–¾in) slit in each cloud, pipe a little white royal icing inside and gently push the large ghosts through and into the cake. Attach the small ghosts around the cakes and the moon to the front of the cake with edible glue. Use black trimmings to make two wispy clouds to go across the moon and attach with a dab of royal icing.

8 **For the spider** Roll 10g (³⁄₈oz) black sugarpaste into a ball and flatten. Attach to the front of the board then pipe legs with black royal icing. Use orange trimmings for the eyes. Make mini spiders by rolling four smaller balls from the black trimmings and attach randomly to the cake using edible glue, adding legs and eyes in the same way.

## Materials

- 12 chocolate cupcakes baked in black cupcake cases
- 600g (1lb 5oz) chocolate buttercream
- 200g (7oz) black sherbet
- Approximately 5m (5yd) liquorice bootlaces cut into 5cm (2in) lengths
- 24 purple, red or orange candy-coated sweets

## Equipment

- Large piping (pastry) bag with a large round tube (tip)
- Shallow dish
- Basic equipment (see Basic Tools and Equipment)

### Jobs that can be done in advance:

☆ Bake the cupcakes (see Classic Vanilla Sponge Cake, chocolate variation, in Recipes)

### Great jobs for the kids:

✪ So easy they can do it all!

# Scary Spider Cupcakes

These scary cupcakes will go down a 'treat' at Halloween parties. Bake the cupcakes in advance, lay out bowls of decorations and bags of icing and let the kids go mad decorating spook-tacular cupcakes!

1 Fill the large piping (pastry) bag with the chocolate buttercream, pipe a mound in the centre of each cupcake and smooth down the sides to create a dome shape.

2 Decant the black sherbet into a shallow dish. Hold the cupcakes upside down and roll in the sherbet until completely covered.

3 Push eight lengths of liquorice into each spider for the legs and use two sweets for the eyes.

*she's not scared of spiders*

# Spooky Skull Cupcakes

These super spooky skull cupcakes are a double treat – yummy cake with a mountain of frosting AND a generous chunk of creamy white chocolate!

1 Melt the Candy Melts according to the instructions on the packet and spoon the melted chocolate into the small piping (pastry) bag. Snip the end off the bag and pipe chocolate into each skull mould. Holding both sides of the mould, lift and tap firmly on the work surface to release any air bubbles. Place in the freezer for 10 minutes to set.

2 Fill a large piping (pastry) bag fitted with a large star tube (tip) with the buttercream. Pipe a swirl of buttercream on top of each cupcake (see Piping and Flooding in Techniques) and drop each cupcake inside a wrapper.

3 To remove the skulls from the moulds, turn upside down and tap firmly. Place a skull in the centre of each cupcake and drop small balls of black sugarpaste into the eye sockets for the eyes.

## Jobs that can be done in advance:

☆ Bake the cupcakes (see Classic Vanilla Sponge Cake, orange variation, in Recipes)
☆ Make the skulls (see Step 1)
☆ Assemble the wrappers (see Step 2)

## Great jobs for the kids:

✪ So easy they can do it all!

## Tip...
Secure the cupcake wrappers with a small square of sticky tape to prevent them popping open.

For the Ghoulish Eyeball Cupcakes shown at the start of the chapter, visit www.bakeme.com/love-this-book to download the project instructions.

*easy squeezy*

# Picnic Party

This is a fantastic cake to make with kids of all ages as they can try their hand at almost every part of it and tend to love all the modelling involved. The hardest bit is trying to stop them eating the tiny picnic food before you've finished putting the cake together!

## Materials

- 30cm (12in) square filled cake, covered with green sugarpaste
- 40cm (16in) square cake drum, covered with green sugarpaste and edged with green ribbon
- Readymade sugardough: 700g (1lb 8⅝oz) light brown
- Sugarpaste: 1.1kg (2lb 6⅞oz) white, 120g (4¼oz) green, 50g (1¾oz) yellow, 22g (¾oz) dark brown, 15g (½oz) mid brown, 8g (¼oz) red, 7g (¼oz) black, 6g (¼oz) bright green, 2g (⅛oz) pink
- Petal paste: 60g (2oz) white, 10g (⅜oz) mid brown
- Royal icing: 45ml (3 tbsp) white, 15ml (1 tbsp) each black, red, yellow, green
- White edible paint
- Black paste food colouring
- Edible glue
- 2 sticks of dried spaghetti, each approximately 8cm (3in) long

## Equipment

- 5 piping (pastry) bags with no.2 tubes (tips)
- Cutters: 4.5cm (1¾in) circle and fluted circle, 3.5cm (1⅜in) circle, small blossom, variety of small flowers
- Paint palette
- Fine paintbrush
- Cocktail stick (toothpick)
- Basic equipment (see Basic Tools and Equipment)

### Jobs that can be done in advance:

☆ Cover the cake and board (see Filling and Covering in Techniques)
☆ Colour the pastes and royal icings
☆ Make the plates (see Step 6)

### Great jobs for the kids:

✪ With a little guidance and patience, they can have a go at it all!

*piping jam is easy!*

*the perfect job for tiny fingers*

# Teddy Bears' Picnic

1 Spread 15ml (1 tbsp) white royal icing in the centre of the board and position the cake squarely on top. Divide 120g (4¼oz) green sugarpaste into four and roll each into a sausage approximately 30cm (12in) long and 8mm (¼in) thick. Secure each sausage around the base of each side of the cake with a line of royal icing, to cover the join between the cake and board. Mitre the corners for a neat finish.

2 **For the tablecloth** Roll out the yellow sugarpaste on a non-stick board lightly dusted with icing (confectioners') sugar and cut out approximately 40 yellow flowers. Reserve the trimmings for the cheese sandwiches. Roll out the white sugarpaste to a 3mm (⅛in) thickness and cut to an approximate 25cm (10in) square, ensuring there is plenty of icing (confectioners') sugar under it at this stage.

3 Lay 25 of the yellow flowers randomly on top of the white sugarpaste and run the rolling pin over the pattern once or twice in both directions to incorporate the flowers into the tablecloth. Moisten the centre of the cake with a damp paintbrush, lift the tablecloth using your rolling pin and drape on top of the cake, on the diagonal, so that the edges hang over the sides. Roll out the white trimmings, cut out 10 white flowers and set aside for later.

4 **For the female teddy** Mould 200g (7oz) of the sugardough into a pear shape for the body and 55g (2oz) into a ball for the head. Insert a stick of spaghetti two-thirds of the way into the bottom of the head to make a hole for later. Remove the spaghetti and insert into the body, leaving 2cm (¾in) showing to support the head. Use 20g (¾oz) for each arm and leg and 4g (⅛oz) for each ear. Use 5g (¼oz) to make a button shape for the nose and mark the face using the wide end of a piping tube (tip) and a knife. Set aside to dry for 10 minutes then assemble using edible glue (see Figure Modelling in Techniques). Using a piping (pastry) bag with a no.2 tube (tip), pipe eyes and a nose using the black royal icing. Finally, roll three small balls from the pink sugarpaste to make a bow and attach to the head with edible glue. Position the bear on the tablecloth on the right-hand side of the cake.

**5** **For the male teddy** Repeat step 4 for the male bear, only using the black sugarpaste to make a bow tie instead of a hair bow. Position him on the tablecloth on the left-hand side of the cake.

**6** **For the plates** Roll out 25g (⅞oz) white petal paste to a 1mm (¹⁄₁₆in) thickness and cut out eight 4.5cm (1¾in) circles and place them in the wells of a paint palette to dry in a cupped shape.

**7** **For the cake stand** Mould 15g (½oz) white petal paste into an egg-timer shape, making sure both ends are flat. Roll out 20g (¾oz) white petal paste to a 5mm (⅛in) thickness and cut out a 4.5cm (1¾in) fluted circle. Set both aside to dry completely then assemble using a dab of royal icing.

**8** **For the cake** Roll out 10g (⅜oz) white sugarpaste trimmings and 10g (⅜oz) dark brown sugarpaste to a 5mm (⅛in) thickness and cut out two 3.5cm (1⅜in) circles from each colour. Stack alternately using a dab of edible glue. Model six tiny strawberries using 3g (⅛oz) red sugarpaste. Prick each strawberry with a cocktail stick (toothpick) to resemble seeds and top with a tiny ball of bright green sugarpaste for the stalk. Attach the strawberries around the edge of the top of the cake with a dab of edible glue. Cut one slice of cake and lay it on the tablecloth. Attach the rest of the cake to the cake stand with a dab of royal icing and set aside.

*Tip...*
*This cake is much easier if you can prepare all your coloured icings and pastes before you start.*

**9** **For the grapes** Roll lots of tiny balls from the remaining bright green sugarpaste and arrange on a plate. Use a tiny amount of the dark brown sugarpaste to make a stalk. Set aside.

**10** **For the jam tarts** Roll out 10g (⅜oz) mid brown petal paste to a 1mm (¹⁄₁₆in) thickness and cut out 12 mini tart cases using the small blossom cutter. Using a piping (pastry) bag with a no.2 tube (tip), pipe red royal icing in the centre for the jam. Set aside.

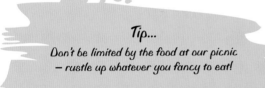

*Tip...*
*Don't be limited by the food at our picnic*
*— rustle up whatever you fancy to eat!*

**11** **For the Swiss roll** Roll out the remaining dark brown sugarpaste to a 2mm (¹⁄₁₆in) thickness into a rectangle measuring 4 x 8cm (1½ x 3⅛in) and dampen with a paintbrush. Roll a slightly smaller rectangle using white sugarpaste trimmings and lay on top of the brown. Roll up to form the Swiss roll, trimming both ends to neaten, and finish by dusting with icing (confectioners') sugar. Cut two slices and place on plates for the bears and place the remaining Swiss roll on another plate and set all aside.

**12** **For the sandwiches** Roll out the remaining white sugarpaste trimmings to a 2mm (¹⁄₁₆in) thickness and cut out two rectangles measuring 4 x 8cm (1½ x 3⅛in). Cut each one in half widthways. From the red and yellow trimmings, cut out two 4cm (1½in) squares and lay each one on top of a white square, dampening with a paintbrush to secure. Top with the remaining white squares and cut into small triangles. Arrange on a plate and set aside.

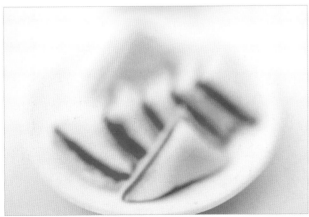

**13** **For the roast chicken** Mould 15g (½oz) mid brown sugarpaste into the chicken's component parts (two drumsticks, two wings and a body) and secure together with edible glue. Attach to a plate and set aside.

**14** Arrange all the plates of food and the cake stand on the tablecloth as shown, securing all items with a little royal icing.

**15** **For the border** Using a piping (pastry) bag with a no.2 tube, pipe green royal icing stems randomly around the sides of the cake and top with the yellow and white flowers set aside earlier, piping contrasting dots in their centres. Pipe grass around the base of the flowers (see Piping and Flooding in Techniques). Paint the dandelions using white edible paint and a fine paintbrush.

**16** **For the ants** Roll 18–20 tiny balls of black sugarpaste and secure one for the head and one for the body of each ant in a line from the edge of the board up the side of the cake and across to the slice of cake on the tablecloth using edible glue. Paint the legs with a fine paintbrush dipped in black paste food colouring.

*Tip...*
It is very useful to invest in a few no.2 piping tubes (tips), as they are so versatile. It also saves having to wash them out each time you change colour.

# Ladybird Whoopie Pies

These cheeky little ladybirds are bound to brighten up any picnic, whatever the weather!

1 Roll out the red sugarpaste to a 2mm (¹⁄₁₆in) thickness and cut out six 10cm (4in) circles. Moisten the undersides with a damp paintbrush and fix on top of the whoopies, smoothing down the sides. Score a line with a knife down the centre of each whoopie to make the wings.

2 Roll out the white sugarpaste to a 4mm (⅛in) thickness and cut out twelve 1cm (⅜in) circles. Roll out the black sugarpaste to a 2mm (¹⁄₁₆in) thickness and cut out three 7cm (2¾in) circles, thirty-six 1cm (⅜in) circles and twelve 5mm (⅛in) circles.

3 Cut the three 7cm (2¾in) black circles in half and position one half at the front of each whoopie, securing with edible glue. Stick two white circles on each black semi-circle for the eyes and use the smallest circles for the pupils. Stick the remaining dots on the ladybirds for spots (six per ladybird).

*how many spots should she have?*

## Materials

- 12 round cookies, 6cm (2⅜in)
- Sugarpaste: 400g (14oz) each yellow, black, 10g (⅜oz) white
- 2 lengths of red liquorice
- Edible glue

## Equipment

- 6cm (2⅜in) round cookie cutter
- Paintbrush
- Basic equipment (see Basic Tools and Equipment)

### Jobs that can be done in advance:

☆ Bake the cookies (see Vanilla Sugar Cookies in Recipes)

### Great jobs for the kids:

✪ So easy they can do it all!

# Buzzy Bumblebee Cookies

Usually, everyone hates insects at picnics, but this time they will all want to be near these cute little bumblebees!

1 Roll out the yellow and black sugarpastes to a 2mm (⅟₁₆in) thickness and cut out twelve 6cm (2⅜in) circles in each colour. Moisten the underside of each yellow circle with a dab of water and stick one on each cookie.

2 Cut each black circle into four equal parts, discarding one of the middle strips. Stick the two curved strips to the top and bottom of the cookie and the straight strip across the centre using a barely damp paintbrush.

3 For each bumblebee, roll two small balls of white sugarpaste for eyes and two tiny black balls for pupils. Cut small lengths of red liquorice for the mouths and attach features to each bumblebee, securing with edible glue.

*a smiley mouth to make you smile*

# Mother's Day Delights

Any mum would love to be presented with this beautifully elegant butterfly cake on her special day. As well as being perfect for Mother's Day, it would also make an ideal birthday cake or a great cake for any time that you just want to say thanks to a wonderful mum!

## Materials

- 25cm (10in) round filled cake covered with white sugarpaste and trimmed with pink ribbon
- 35cm (14in) round cake drum covered with pink sugarpaste and edged with pink ribbon
- Petal paste: 20g (3/4oz) each white, green, yellow, pink, blue
- Edible glitter: white hologram, electric lime, pastel lemon, pastel pink, disco baby blue
- 30ml (2 tbsp) royal icing

## Equipment

- Butterfly cutters: large and small
- Large piece of card
- Small paintbrush
- Piping (pastry) bag with a no.2 tube (tip)
- Pink ribbon, 86cm (34in) long
- Basic equipment (see Basic Tools and Equipment)

### Jobs that can be done in advance:

☆ Cover the cake and board (see Filling and Covering in Techniques)
☆ Make the butterflies (see Step 1)

### Great jobs for the kids:

✪ So easy they can do it all!

*beautiful butterflies*

*gently does it*

# Dazzling Butterfly Cake

1 The day before you want to decorate your cake, make your butterflies, as they need at least 24 hours to dry completely and hold their shape. Roll out the petal pastes to a 1mm (1/16in) thickness and cut approximately four large and two small butterflies from each colour. Dry each butterfly by resting it over a folded piece of card for 24 hours.

2 When completely dry, moisten the butterflies with a damp paintbrush and sprinkle liberally with the corresponding colour of edible glitter.

3 Spread 15ml (1 tbsp) royal icing in the centre of the covered cake board, position the cake in the middle and trim with pink ribbon (see Trimming a Cake and Board with Ribbon in Techiques).

4 Pipe a thin line of royal icing on the underside of each butterfly and attach randomly to the cake.

*Tip...*
*Use the box your sugarpaste came in or*
*an old cereal box to dry your butterflies.*

## Materials

- 12 vanilla cupcakes, baked in pink cupcake cases
- 600g (1lb 7¼oz) vanilla buttercream, coloured pink
- Petal paste: 30g (1oz) white
- 15ml (1 tbsp) pink royal icing

## Equipment

- Medium daisy cutter
- Small shallow dish or paint palette
- Large piping (pastry) bag with a large round tube (tip)
- Small piping (pastry) bag with a no.2 tube (tip)
- Basic equipment (see Basic Tools and Equipment)

### Jobs that can be done in advance:

☆ Bake the cupcakes (see Classic Vanilla Sponge Cake in Recipes)
☆ Make the daisies (see Step 1)

### Great jobs for the kids:

✪ So easy they can do it all!

# Darling Daisy Cupcakes

Pink fluffy icing swirled high on top of a cupcake – the key to any mum's heart!

**1** Roll out the petal paste to a 1mm (¹⁄₁₆in) thickness and cut out 12 daisies. Place each in a small shallow dish or paint palette to dry in a cupped shaped. Leave to dry for a few hours or overnight.

**2** Using a large piping (pastry) bag with a large round tube (tip), pipe a swirl of buttercream on top of each cupcake (see Piping and Flooding in Techniques) and place a daisy in the centre.

**3** Using a small piping (pastry) bag with a no.2 tube (tip), pipe dots of royal icing in the centre of each daisy.

*the perfect daughters...*

## Materials

- 8 large flower-shaped cookies
- 1 vase-shaped cookie
- Royal icing: 15ml (1 tbsp) each blue, pink, yellow; 30ml (2 tbsp) each white, green
- Flooding icing: 45ml (3 tbsp) each blue, green, yellow, pink; 60ml (4 tbsp) white
- 45cm (18in) square cake drum covered with pale blue sugarpaste and edged with pale blue ribbon
- Petal paste: 5g (¼oz) white

## Equipment

- Large flower cookie cutter
- Vase template (see Templates)
- 5 piping (pastry) bags with no.2 tubes (tips) (for the royal icing)
- 5 piping (pastry) bags without tubes (tips) (for the flooding icing)
- Small daisy cutter
- Cocktail stick (toothpick)
- Basic equipment (see Basic Tools and Equipment)

## Blooming Bouquet Cookies

What could be better? A handmade bouquet to go with mum's beautiful cake – and you can even eat the vase!

**1 For the flowers** Outline and flood the flower cookies in matching colours (see Piping and Flooding in Techniques) (two cookies per colour). Allow to dry completely (preferably overnight) then outline the cookies again with white royal icing.

**2 For the vase** Roll out the petal paste to a 1mm (1/16in) thickness and cut out 12–15 small daisies. Pipe centres with the yellow royal icing. Outline and flood the vase using the same technique as step 1. While the flooding icing is still wet, drop the daisies into the icing at regular intervals to make a pattern for the vase. Set aside to dry completely (preferably overnight).

**3 Position** the vase at the bottom of the board and secure using a few dots of royal icing. Stick the flower cookies above the vase in the same way and use the green royal icing to pipe stems from each flower to the vase, or to the flower below.

## Jobs that can be done in advance:

- ☆ Bake the cookies (see Vanilla Sugar Cookies in Recipes)
- ☆ Make the daisies (see Step 1)
- ☆ Colour the icings (making sure you cover well with cling film/plastic wrap to avoid crusting)

## Great jobs for the kids:

- ✪ Cut the flower shapes
- ✪ Flood the vase and flowers with icing (see Steps 1–2)
- ✪ Make the daisies (see Step 2)

### Tip...
*Use the cocktail stick (toothpick) to pull the flooding icing right into the edges.*

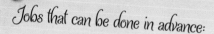

# Gifts for Teachers

This delicious apple cake is the perfect way to get into your teacher's good books at the end of term. The shape of the cake may look difficult to achieve but it is carved from a template and is actually very easy. Spend time getting a smooth shape to give you a lovely juicy apple!

## Materials

- 30cm (12in) round cake in the flavour of your choice, filled but not crumb coated
- 35cm (14in) square cake drum covered with red sugarpaste and edged with red ribbon
- 300g (10½oz) buttercream in the flavour of your choice
- Sugarpaste: 1.5kg (3lb 5oz) green
- Petal paste: 3g (⅛oz) black
- Green paste food colouring
- 1.25ml (¼ tsp) CMC (Tylo) powder
- 15ml (1 tbsp) royal icing
- Edible glue
- 1 twig-shaped snack (such as a pretzel or Twiglet)

## Equipment

- Apple template (see Templates)
- Piping (pastry) bag with a no.2 tube (tip)
- Paintbrush
- Piping tube (tip) – any size
- Small sharp knife
- Small length of dried spaghetti (approx 4cm/1½in long)
- Basic equipment (see Basic Tools and Equipment)

### Jobs that can be done in advance:

☆ Cover the board (see Filling and Covering in Techniques)
☆ Colour the paste
☆ Make the worm (see Steps 1–4)

### Great jobs for the kids:

✪ Colour the paste
✪ Make the worm (see Steps 1–4)
✪ Eat the leftover pretzels!

*this definitely deserves a grade A!*

*stop wriggling!*

# Apple for the Teacher Cake

**1 For the worm** Remove 20g (¾oz) green sugarpaste and colour it a darker green, incorporating the CMC (Tylo) powder. Roll into a bent sausage shape measuring approximately 6 x 2cm (2⅜ x ¾in) and push the spaghetti up through the bottom of the sausage, leaving 2cm (¾in) protruding.

**2** Using a piping (pastry) bag with a no.2 tube (tip), pipe two round dots of royal icing for eyes, leave to dry for a few minutes, then stick tiny balls of black petal paste on top for the pupils. Use the edge of a piping tube (tip) to indent a smile.

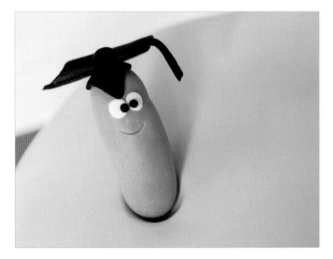

**3** Roll out the black petal paste to a 1mm (¹⁄₁₆in) thickness and cut out a diamond shape, each side measuring approximately 2cm (¾in) for the cap of the mortar board. Glue across the top of the worm's head, with the longer points at the front and back, then set aside to dry.

**4** Re-roll the remaining black petal paste and cut a 4cm (1½in) square for the mortar board and from the trimmings, roll a thin sausage approximately 4cm (1½in) long for the tassel. Fringe one end of this using a sharp knife and stick the unfringed end in the centre of the mortar board, gluing a tiny ball of black petal paste on top to hide the join. Set the mortar board aside to dry, ensuring the tassel is suspended so that it doesn't break.

*Tip...*
*Pipe a personal greeting in the centre of the cake for your special teacher.*

**5 For the apple** Carve the cake into an apple shape using the template (see Carving in Techniques). Crumb coat the carved cake with the buttercream, then cover with the green sugarpaste (see Filling and Covering in Techniques). Make an indent in the cake with your thumb for the worm. Squeeze a little royal icing into the indent then place the worm in the hole, pushing the spaghetti firmly into the cake at the same time.

**6** Attach the mortar board to the worm's head with royal icing. Squeeze the remaining royal icing in the centre of the covered cake board then carefully lift the cake using a cake lifter and position centrally on the board. Finally, insert the twig-shaped snack into the top of the apple for the stalk.

*Tip...*
*If you don't manage to trim the sugarpaste at the bottom of your cake very neatly, you can always edge it with ribbon and no one will know!*

## Materials

- 1 quantity vanilla sugar cookie dough
- Sugarpaste: 120g (4½oz) each, red, green, yellow; 30g (1oz) grey
- Royal icing: 5ml (1 tsp) each, red, green, yellow; 15ml (1 tbsp) each white, grey
- 5 marshmallows

## Equipment

- Ruler template (see Templates)
- 3 small bowls
- 2 piping (pastry) bags with no.2 tubes (tips)
- Basic equipment (see Basic Tools and Equipment)

### Jobs that can be done in advance:

☆ Bake the cookies (see Vanilla Sugar Cookies in Recipes)
☆ Colour the icings

### Great jobs for the kids:

❂ Roll and cut the dough (see Step 1)
❂ Dip the pencils (see Step 3)
❂ Roll the paste (see Steps 4 and 6)

### Tip...
*Dip the pencils in grey royal icing instead of coloured icings to make lead pencils.*

# Smart Stationery Cookies

Chewing the end of your pencil has never been so tasty!

**1** Divide the cookie dough in half, roll out one half to around 4mm (⅛in) thick and cut out nine rulers using the template. Use the other half to roll nine sausages approximately 16cm (6¼in) long x 2cm (¾in) wide and pinch at one end to make pencil points. Lay on baking trays and refrigerate for an hour before baking in an oven, preheated to 180°C (350°F / Gas 4) for 10–12 minutes. Remove from the oven, transfer to a wire rack and allow to cool completely before decorating.

**2** **For the rulers** Using a piping (pastry) bag with a no.2 tube (tip), pipe grey royal icing markings along one edge of each ruler, using the template as a guide.

**3** **For the pencils** In separate bowls, water down the red, yellow and green royal icings to a runny consistency and dip the points of three pencils in each colour icing. Allow to dry.

**4** Roll out the red sugarpaste to a 2mm (¹⁄₁₆in) thickness and cut out three 14 x 4cm (5½ x 1½in) rectangles. Lightly brush the undersides of the paste with water, drape over the cookies with the red tips and trim to fit. Use your hands to smooth the paste. Repeat with the yellow and green pastes and pencils.

**5** Cut the marshmallows in half vertically and rub the cut edges in a little icing (confectioners') sugar. Using a piping (pastry) bag with a no.2 tube (tip), pipe a little white royal icing on the end of the pencils and attach the marshmallows, cut-side down.

**6** Roll out the grey sugarpaste and cut nine 2 x 5cm (¾ x 2in) strips. Mark lines on the strips at regular intervals with the back of a knife. Pipe a zigzag of white royal icing over the join between the marshmallow and pencil and lay the grey strips over the top to hide the joins, tucking the ends underneath.

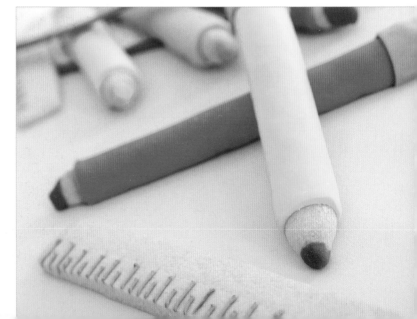

## Materials

- 15 cake pops on sticks
- 1 packet red Candy Melts (400g/14oz)
- Green liquorice, approximately 15cm (6in)

## Equipment

- Tall thin microwaveable container
- Florists' oasis or polystyrene block
- Basic equipment (see Basic Tools and Equipment)

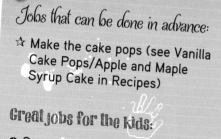

## Jobs that can be done in advance:

☆ Make the cake pops (see Vanilla Cake Pops/Apple and Maple Syrup Cake in Recipes)

## Great jobs for the kids:

✪ So easy they can do it all!

# Toffee Apple Cake Pops

A fun and delicious alternative to the traditional 'apple for the teacher'.

1 Melt the Candy Melts in a tall thin microwaveable container, following the instructions on the packet.

2 Cut the liquorice into 1cm (⅜in) lengths and set aside.

3 Dip each cake pop completely into the melted chocolate, remove, then tap the stick gently on the side of the container to remove any excess chocolate, twisting the stick slowly as you do so.

4 Push the cake pop into the oasis or polystyrene and then immediately push a length of liquorice into the top for the stalk, while the chocolate is still runny. Repeat the process for the remaining cake pops and leave to set.

### Tip...

*Place your cake pops in a clean jam jar and tie with cellophane and pretty ribbon or a in a cake pop presentation box, for the perfect gift.*

*master of disguise!*

# Summer Fair

Schools are always on the lookout for fabulous raffle prizes for the summer fête and what better way to contribute than to donate this gorgeous two-tiered polka-dot cake? While it looks spectacular, it is so easy to make and is sure to be the most coveted prize on the raffle table!

## Materials

- 20cm (8in) and 25cm (10in) round filled cakes, covered with white sugarpaste
- 35cm (14in) round cake drum covered with fuchsia sugarpaste and edged with white ribbon
- Sugarpaste: 100g (3½oz) fuchsia, 100g (3½oz) lime green (made using leaf green and a touch of egg yellow), 30g (1oz) white
- 30ml (2 tbsp) royal icing
- White hologram edible glitter
- Edible glue

## Equipment

- 5 plastic dowels
- Round cutters: varying small sizes from 5mm–2cm (⅛–¾in)
- 4 lengths of white florists' wire
- Small posy pick
- Paintbrush
- Ribbon: 157cm (62in) each white and narrow fuchsia
- Basic equipment (see Basic Tools and Equipment)

### Jobs that can be done in advance:

- ☆ Cover the cakes and board (see Filling and Covering in Techniques)
- ☆ Stack the cakes (see Dowelling in Techniques)

### Great jobs for the kids:

- ✪ Cut, glitter and stick the dots (see Steps 3–5)
- ✪ Roll and glitter the balls (see Steps 6–7)

*goodness, gracious, great balls of icing!*

*she's a bit dotty*

# First-Prize Raffle Cake

1 Spread 15ml (1 tbsp) royal icing in the centre of the covered cake board, position the 25cm (10in) cake on the board making sure it is nicely centred and dowel the cake (see Dowelling in Techniques).

2 Spread the remainder of the royal icing in the centre of the 25cm (10in) cake on top of the dowels, and then carefully drop the 20cm (8in) cake on top, again taking care to position it centrally.

3 Set aside 10g (⅜oz) of each colour sugarpaste for later. Roll out the remaining fuchsia sugarpaste to a 2mm (¹⁄₁₆in) thickness onto a non-stick board dusted with a little icing (confectioners') sugar to avoid sticking. Cut polka dots of varying sizes using the round cutters, and set aside one of the large fuchsia dots for later.

4 Repeat the process described in step 3 to make green polka dots. Finally, roll out the white sugarpaste and cut a few 5mm (⅛in) circles. Moisten these with a barely damp paintbrush and sprinkle with white edible glitter.

*Tip...*
*Beware – if too much edible glue is used, the dots may slide down the cake and the colours might run all over your lovely white icing.*

5 Stick all the polka dots randomly on the cakes, using a paintbrush and the smallest amount of edible glue. Make sure to leave an empty space in the centre of the top cake for the wire spray.

6 Half fill the posy pick with a small ball of white sugarpaste to anchor the wires, then push the pick into the centre of the cake until it is level with the surface. Using the remaining sugarpastes, roll seven balls. Cut each wire in half and bend one end of each wire to make a small hook. Dip the hooks in edible glue and insert one into each ball.

7 Moisten only the white balls with a barely damp paintbrush and dip in edible white glitter to make them sparkle. Arrange the wires in the posy pick by cutting to varying lengths and pushing firmly into the sugarpaste.

8 Make a small cut in the centre of the remaining fuchsia polka dot and carefully position around the wires and covering the top of the pick for a neat finish.

## Materials

- 24 cereal cupcakes baked in white cupcake cases
- 1.2kg (2lb 10¼oz) vanilla buttercream
- Paste food colouring: orange, green, purple and pink
- Fruity loop-shaped cereal (such as Froot Loops) to decorate

## Equipment

- 4 large piping (pastry) bags with large star tubes (tips)
- Basic equipment (see Basic Tools and Equipment)

# Lovely Loopy Cupcakes

These eye-catching cupcakes are particularly easy to decorate, but are guaranteed to draw a crowd around the summer fair bake stall.

1 Divide the buttercream into four equal portions. Colour one portion orange, spoon into a piping (pastry) bag with a large star tube (tip) and pipe a swirl of buttercream on top of six of the cupcakes (see Piping and Flooding in Techniques).

2 Repeat with the remaining buttercream until you have six cupcakes in each colour.

3 Decorate each cupcake with a handful of fruity loop-shaped cereal.

*Jobs that can be done in advance:*

☆ Bake the cupcakes (see Cereal Cupcakes in Recipes)
☆ Colour the buttercream

**Great jobs for the kids:**

❁ So easy they can do it all!

*my turn next!*

## Materials

- 200g (7oz) white chocolate, melted
- 200g (7oz) milk chocolate, melted
- Colourful edible sprinkles

## Equipment

- Lollipop mould
- 12 lollipop sticks
- 12 acetate bags
- Ribbon
- Basic equipment (see Basic Tools and Equipment)

### Jobs that can be done in advance:

☆ Gather the equipment

### Great jobs for the kids:

✪ So easy they can do it all!

# Giant Chocolate Lollipops

These lovely lollipops will sell like hot cakes on the baked goods stall, bagged and tied with brightly coloured ribbon – if your kids don't eat them all first!

1 Scatter a handful of sprinkles into each mould. Place the sticks in the wells and spoon or pour melted chocolate to fill each mould, ensuring the sticks are well covered. Tap gently to remove any air bubbles and refrigerate for approximately 30 minutes or until set and firm.

2 To release the lollipops, twist the moulds very gently until they pop out. Store in a cool place until needed then place individually in acetate bags and tie with ribbon.

**Tip...**
Be careful not to twist the mould too vigorously to release the lollipops as they may crack.

*I'll make them, you eat them*

# Rainy-Day Fun

Getting out the paints and creating a work of art is always a great activity on a grey day. But here's an even better idea – get your budding little Picassos to make you an edible version instead! This fantastic project is suitable for all ages – and what a surprise when you discover the masterpiece within the cake...

## Materials

- Prepared batter for a 20cm (8in) vanilla sponge cake (see Recipes)
- Paste food colouring: red, yellow, blue, green, orange
- Sugarpaste: 1.25kg (2lb 12oz) white
- 100g (3½oz) vanilla buttercream
- 30cm (12in) round cake drum covered with white sugarpaste and edged with white ribbon
- Royal icing: 15ml (1 tbsp) each white, red, orange, yellow, green, blue, purple

## Equipment

- 6 small bowls
- 5 medium-sized bowls
- 20cm (8in) round cake tin (pan), greased and lined
- 20cm (8in) thin round cake board
- 6 teaspoons
- White ribbon, 71cm (28in) long
- Basic equipment (see Basic Tools and Equipment)

*great job kids!*

### Jobs that can be done in advance:

☆ Cover the cake and board (see Filling and Covering in Techniques)
☆ Colour the royal icing

### Great jobs for the kids:

✪ So easy they can do it all!

*artists at work*

# Crazy Splatter Cake

1 To make the cake, divide the batter equally between the five medium-sized bowls and colour each one separately using the paste food colourings.

2 Spoon the first colour into the centre of the tin (pan), being careful not to spread it out, then carefully spoon the second colour onto the centre of the first colour (again, not spreading the batter manually). Repeat with remaining coloured batters. Rather magically, the colours spread in concentric circles to the edge of the tin (pan).

3 Transfer to the oven and bake as per the recipe instructions (see Classic Vanilla Sponge Cake in Recipes). Remove from the oven and allow to cool completely before decorating.

4 To decorate, spread 15ml (1 tbsp) buttercream in the centre of the thin board and place the cake upside down on the board. Crumb coat the cake using the remaining buttercream (see Filling and Covering in Techniques) and cover with cling film (plastic wrap) to prevent the crumb coat from drying.

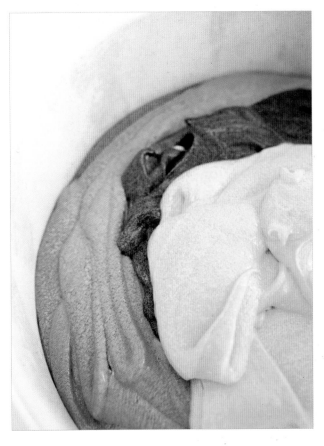

*Tip...*

*This splatter cake is also fabulous for a birthday celebration, especially if you are having a paintballing or ceramic-painting party!*

5 Roll out the white sugarpaste, remove the cling film (plastic wrap) and cover the cake (see Filling and Covering in Techniques).

6 Spread the white royal icing in the centre of the covered board and position the cake in the centre.

7 Place each of the coloured royal icings into a small bowl and thin down each coloured icing with a little water until you have a soft dropping consistency. Be careful to add water drop by drop as a little water goes a long way.

8 Using a clean teaspoon for each colour, dribble the icings all over the cake and board to create your own individual masterpiece! When the icing is dry, trim the cake with the white ribbon (see Trimming a Cake and Board with Ribbon in Techniques).

*Tip...*
*You might want to wait until the splatters have dried before you edge the board with ribbon too.*

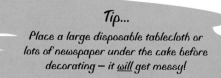
*Tip...*
*Place a large disposable tablecloth or lots of newspaper under the cake before decorating — it will get messy!*

## Materials

- 24 cupcakes in the flavour and cases of your choice
- 1.5kg (3lb 5oz) vanilla buttercream
- Paste food colouring: orange, pink, green, blue
- Edible sprinkles

## Equipment

- 5 medium-sized bowls
- 4 large piping (pastry) bags with large star tubes (tips)
- Cake plate or stand to display
- Basic equipment (see Basic Tools and Equipment)

### Jobs that can be done in advance:

☆ Bake the cupcakes (see Classic Vanilla Sponge Cake in Recipes)
☆ Colour the buttercream

### Great jobs for the kids:

✪ Filling the piping (pastry) bags is a bit fiddly, so probably not suitable for younger children, but once this is done, even the youngest children can ice the cakes and decorate with sprinkles

*sprinkling is my job!*

# Psychedelic Cupcakes

These colourful swirly cupcakes complement the rainbow cake perfectly – a cheery antidote to a rainy day!

1 Divide the buttercream equally between four medium-sized bowls and colour each one separately using the paste food colourings.

2 Lay one piping (pastry) bag on its side on a flat surface, and spoon half the pink buttercream into the bag, taking care to push the icing right down towards the tube (tip) and to keep it away from the top half of the bag as far as possible. Spoon half the orange buttercream in the remaining space – also taking care to push the icing all the way down to the tube (tip).

3 Twist the top of the bag to compress the icing at the point then pipe a few centimetres of icing into the spare bowl – this will remove any air at the top of the bag, and also help to ensure that both icing colours have reached the end of the tube (tip).

4 Pipe a two-tone swirl on top of six cupcakes (see Piping and Flooding in Techniques) and decorate with sprinkles.

5 Repeat with different two-colour buttercream combinations for the remaining cupcakes.

## Materials

- 12 teaspoon-shaped cookies
- 30ml (2 tbsp) grey royal icing
- 90ml (6 tbsp) grey flooding icing
- 30g (2 tbsp) Demerara (golden granulated) sugar

## Equipment

- Teaspoon-shaped cookie cutter or template (see Templates)
- Piping (pastry) bag with a no.2 tube (tip)
- Piping (pastry) bag (without tube/tip)
- Basic equipment (see Basic Tools and Equipment)

### Jobs that can be done in advance:

☆ Bake the cookies (see Vanilla Sugar Cookies in Recipes)

### Great jobs for the kids:

✪ So easy they can do it all!

# Sugar Spoon Cookies

While lots of children splattering and swirling with brightly coloured icing is enormous fun, it does make a bit of a mess! Once you've cleaned up, reward yourself with one of these gorgeous cookies and a nice cup of tea...

1 Outline and flood the cookies using the grey icings (see Piping and Flooding in Techniques).

2 Before the flooding icing sets, sprinkle the bowl of each teaspoon cookie with Demerara (golden granulated) sugar.

3 Enjoy with a lovely cup of tea!

*I know where to put this sugar...*

# Be My Valentine

This incredible creation will melt the heart of any chocoholic on Valentine's Day. It is the perfect romantic gift for your sweetheart, which the kids can help you to make – or if you are lucky parents, they can make it for the two of you!

## Materials

- 20cm (8in) round chocolate cake, filled and crumb coated with chocolate ganache and covered with cling film (plastic wrap)
- 500g (1lb 1½oz) chocolate cigarillos
- Petal paste: 5g (¼oz) red
- Large box of chocolates

## Equipment

- Small heart cutter
- Pretty ribbon and bow
- Non-toxic glue stick
- Pretty plate or cake stand
- Basic equipment (see Basic Tools and Equipment)

### Jobs that can be done in advance:

☆ Bake the cake (see Classic Vanilla Sponge Cake, chocolate variation in Recipes)

☆ Make the chocolate ganache (see Fillings and Toppings)

☆ Fill and crumb coat the cake (see Filling and Covering in Techniques)

### Great jobs for the kids:

✪ So easy they can do it all!

*made with love*

*chocolate... yum!*

# Chocolate Heaven Cake

1 Roll out the petal paste to a 1mm (1/16in) thickness and cut out a few small hearts. Allow to dry.

2 Place the cake in the centre of your serving plate or cake stand and remove the cling film (plastic wrap). Stick the cigarillos all around the outside, positioning them as close to each other as possible.

3 Wrap the ribbon around the cake and secure the ends to each other using the non-toxic glue stick. Attach the bow to cover the join. As well as looking beautiful, this will help to keep the cigarillos firmly in place.

4 Pile chocolates all over the top of the cake and scatter the hearts amongst the chocolates.

*Tip...*
*Covering your cake with cling film (plastic wrap) keeps the crumb coat moist so that the cigarillos stick more easily. If your crumb coat does dry and your cigarillos fall off, simply spread a little extra ganache around the cake and re-stick.*

## Materials

- 100g (3½oz) hoop-shaped cereal (such as Cheerios)
- 200g (7oz) milk chocolate, melted
- Sugarpaste: 120g (4¼oz) red
- 6 edible gold balls

## Equipment

- 6-heart silicone mould
- Basic equipment (see Basic Tools and Equipment)

### Jobs that can be done in advance:

☆ Make the cereal hearts (see Step 1)

☆ Make the bows (see Steps 2–3)

### Great jobs for the kids:

✪ So easy they can do it all!

# Cheery Chocolate Hearts

A great project for even the youngest of children, these lovely little treats look gorgeous wrapped in cellophane and tied with a pretty ribbon and a romantic message.

1 Mix the cereal well with the melted chocolate and pack tightly into the silicone moulds. Reserve a tiny amount of chocolate for sticking the ribbons. Place the filled moulds in the fridge for an hour to set then carefully remove the hearts by gently twisting the mould.

2 Roll out the sugarpaste to a 2mm (⅟₁₆in) thickness and cut six strips approximately 12 x 1.5cm (4¾ x ½in) and six strips approximately 9 x 2cm (3½ x ¾in).

3 For the ribbons, lay the longer strips diagonally across the hearts and secure with a dot of melted chocolate. For the bows, fold both ends of the shorter strips into the centre and pinch to form a bow. Secure to the ribbon with a dot of melted chocolate and push an edible gold ball into the centre of each bow.

*think we need more chocolate*

## Materials

- 12–15 heart-shaped cookies
- 400g (14oz) buttercream
- 5ml (1 tsp) red paste food colouring

## Equipment

- Assorted heart cutters
- Large piping (pastry) bag with large star tube (tip)
- Basic equipment (see Basic Tools and Equipment)

# We ♥ Cookies

While these Valentine heart cookies are stunning to look at (and obviously delicious to eat!), they are so simple to make that apart from using the oven, the kids could make them entirely on their own.

**1** Colour your buttercream by stirring in the red paste food colouring and mixing well. Spoon into the piping (pastry) bag.

**2** Pipe stars all around the edge of each cookie (see Piping and Filling in Techniques). If desired, continue piping stars until the cookies are completely covered.

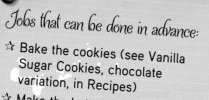

### Jobs that can be done in advance:

- ☆ Bake the cookies (see Vanilla Sugar Cookies, chocolate variation, in Recipes)
- ☆ Make the buttercream (see Fillings and Toppings)

### Great jobs for the kids:

- ❂ Cut the heart shapes
- ❂ Colour the buttercream
- ❂ Pipe the stars (see Piping and Flooding in Techniques)

### Tip...
*Make sure your buttercream is nice and soft for easy piping. If too firm, pop it in the microwave for a few seconds at a time and stir before filling the piping (pastry) bag.*

# Techniques

# Filling and Covering

It is easy to make cakes that look perfect, provided that you take a little care with the early stages of cutting and filling. The recipes in this book make cakes that are deep enough to cut into three layers, which means two layers of filling, helping to keep the cakes lovely and moist for up to four days.

## Materials
### (for a 20cm/8in round cake)

- Cake in the flavour of your choice
- 750g (1lb 10½oz) buttercream
- 175g (6oz) jam (optional)
- Icing (confectioners') sugar for dusting
- Sugarpaste: 1.25kg (2lb 12oz) for the cake; 1kg (2lb 3¼oz) for the board

## Equipment

- 20cm (8in) thin board
- Long serrated knife
- Cake lifter
- Palette/flat knife
- Large plastic rolling pin
- Small sharp knife
- Icing smoother
- Cling film (plastic wrap)
- 30cm (12in) cake drum
- 2 lengths of ribbon, each approximately 2.5cm (1in) longer than the circumference of the board and cake
- Non-toxic glue stick
- Basic equipment (see Basic Tools and Equipment)

# Filling and Crumb Coating a Cake

1 Place your cake upside down on a thin board of the same size and secure with a smear of buttercream. Turning the cake upside down before covering gives a lovely flat surface for icing later on, while the thin board underneath makes the cake much easier to manage when positioning on your iced board, and is also necessary if you are planning to stack your cakes (see Dowelling).

2 As long as you have a steady hand, a reasonably good eye and a long serrated knife, it is fairly straightforward to cut your cake into three using a slow sawing action, keeping an eye on the opposite side of the cake to ensure the knife remains level. However, if you are not confident enough to try this, there are a number of cake levellers and cutters on the market that will help you.

### Tip...
*If your cake is a different size or shape, turn to the table in the Quantity Adjustments section. You will also need a thin cake board the same size as your cake and a cake drum at least 10cm (4in) larger than your cake.*

**3** If you are filling a round cake, indent a couple of converging lines on the side of the cake – this is to ensure that once you have filled a layer, you replace the next layer in exactly the same place, by lining up the indents. This helps to keep the final cake flat, and avoids any problems caused by wonky cutting!

**4** To fill your cake, slide a cake lifter between the bottom and middle layers, and remove the two upper layers. Spread the buttercream evenly and smoothly across the whole bottom layer. It is very important to make sure your buttercream is soft enough for spreading before you start, otherwise it will not stick to your cake. In warm weather, room temperature is usually fine, but in cooler months, you may find you need to give the buttercream a few seconds in the microwave to soften it sufficiently for spreading.

*lines help with re-positioning*

**5** If you are adding jam, spread a layer over the buttercream at this point.

**6** Replace the two upper layers, making sure to line up the indents you cut earlier. Next, slide your lifter between the middle and top layers and repeat the process.

**7** Finally, you will need to crumb coat your cake. To do this, spread a thin layer of buttercream over the sides and top of the cake using a flat knife to give a smooth surface for icing. If you are not covering the cake with sugarpaste immediately, cover the cake with cling film (plastic wrap) to avoid the crumb coat drying out. If this happens, the sugarpaste will not stick to the cake, however it is easily remedied by spreading another thin layer of buttercream round the top and sides, just before covering.

# Covering a Cake with Sugarpaste

**1** Thoroughly clean your work surface of crumbs and grease then sprinkle liberally with icing (confectioners') sugar. Knead your sugarpaste until soft and pliable, and then roll out to a 3mm (⅛in) thickness using a large plastic rolling pin, to a size approximately 13cm (5in) larger all round than the diameter of your cake. Regularly turn the paste through 90 degrees as you roll, and sprinkle icing (confectioners') sugar under the paste to prevent it from sticking.

**2** Once your sugarpaste is the right size, position your rolling pin in the centre of your paste, flip the top half of the paste back over your rolling pin, lift up and drape over your cake.

**3** Use your hands to smooth down the sides, lifting and manipulating the paste until you have a good fit all round.

**4** Trim the excess with a knife and finish off by running an icing smoother across the top and round the sides of the cake to give a lovely smooth finish.

**5** Spread 15ml (1 tbsp) royal icing in the centre of your iced cake drum (see Covering a Board with Sugarpaste). Slide the cake to the edge of your work surface using the smoother and use the thin board under the cake to lift and position it centrally on the iced board.

# Covering a Board with Sugarpaste

**1** Roll out your sugarpaste to a 2mm (¹⁄₁₆in) thickness approximately 2.5cm (1in) larger all round than the diameter of your board.

**2** Moisten the board all over with a few drops of water and transfer the paste to the board in the same way as covering a cake (see Step 2 of Covering a Cake with Sugarpaste). Roll your rolling pin gently over the board to smooth it.

**3** Lift the board in one hand and with the other, trim the excess sugarpaste by running a small sharp knife closely to the edge and cutting downwards, twisting the board as you go. Ideally leave to dry overnight before decorating.

# Trimming a Cake and Board with Ribbon

**1** Measure and cut two lengths of ribbon, each approximately 2.5cm (1in) longer than the circumference of the board and the cake.

**2** To trim the board, run a non-toxic glue stick all around the edge of the board and attach the ribbon, fixing the overlap with a further dab of glue.

**3** Trim the cake once it is fixed onto the covered board. Fix the ribbon around the cake securing with a dab of royal icing at the back. Ensure that the join in the ribbons of both the cake and the board line up at the back.

## Colouring Sugarpaste and Petal Paste

Sugarpaste and petal-paste can be coloured to any shade you desire using the following method.

**1** Knead the paste until soft and pliable.

**2** Dip a cocktail stick (toothpick) into a pot of paste food colouring and transfer to the paste. Knead the paste well until all of the colour has been incorporated and there are no streaks. For a stronger, deeper colour, use more paste food colouring but be aware that a little goes a very long way!

**3** If you are not using it immediately, wrap the paste tightly in cling film (plastic wrap) and store in a plastic bag.

# Carving

Many people are put off by the thought of carving a cake, but it can actually be very straightforward, as long as you prepare well and have the correct tools. The internet is a rich source of templates – type in anything, and hundreds of images will come back, which can be printed, enlarged and traced onto greaseproof (wax) paper for carving (as long as they are copyright free). Of course, you can always draw freehand too! It is also a good idea to make your cake to a size and shape that fits the template best and reduces wastage – although you will find that children are always happy to eat any offcuts!

## Materials

- 30cm (12in) cake in the flavour of your choice – filled, but not crumb coated
- 60ml (4 tbsp) buttercream for crumb coating and sticking

## Equipment

- Small, sharp, non-serrated knife
- Cake lifter or large spatula
- Templates
- Basic equipment (see Basic Tools and Equipment)

**1** Lay your template onto the top of the cake and hold firmly with one hand to avoid slipping. Holding your knife vertically, cut down into the cake, following the line of the template. As you cut round the cake, keep checking that the template hasn't moved. Once you have finished cutting, remove the template and tidy up any loose bits of cake using your knife.

**2** Crumb coat the carved shape as normal (see Filling and Crumb Coating a Cake).

**3** Carved cakes are covered in the same way as regular cakes (see Covering a Cake with Sugarpaste), although you may need to use your hands more to smooth the icing into any dips and crevices. As the cake has been carved, it will not fit neatly onto a thin round or square board for lifting, so we recommend you lift it using a cake lifter or large spatula to position it on your iced board. In this instance, you should also use buttercream rather than royal icing to stick your cake to the board, as this will hold your cake in position much better.

*Tip...*
*Knead the sugarpaste well before rolling out –*
*this will make it softer and more forgiving, so*
*it will be easier to smooth round any curves.*

**4** Trimming an oddly shaped cake with ribbon is also more challenging so take extra care when cutting the sugarpaste at the base of the cake, to eliminate the need to use ribbon. However, if you prefer to trim your cakes with ribbon, just add tiny dots of royal icing at key points to hold your ribbon in place – not too much though, as the moisture from the royal icing can show through the ribbon and spoil the final look of your cake.

# Dowelling

Dowelling is imperative if you are planning to stack one or more cakes on top of each other. If you don't dowel, your top cake will slowly sink into the lower cake and all your hard work will be ruined. Dowelling is very simple if you follow a few basic guidelines.

## Materials

- 2 or more filled and covered cakes (see Filling and Covering) each on thin cake boards the same size as the cakes
- Covered cake board (see Filling and Covering)
- Edible ink pen
- 15ml (1 tbsp) royal icing

## Equipment

- Dowelling template (see Templates)
- Plastic dowels (five per tier)
- Small piece of sandpaper
- Sharp, non-serrated knife
- Basic equipment (see Basic Tools and Equipment)

**1** Place the dowelling template on top of your base tier. If you are stacking a 20cm (8in) round cake onto a 25cm (10in) round cake, mark the holes for the dowels using the yellow dots inside the 20cm (8in) circle, and if you are stacking a 15cm (6in) round cake onto a 20cm (8in) round cake, mark the holes for the dowels using the yellow dots inside the 15cm (6in) circle. Similarly, If you are stacking a 20cm (8in) square cake onto a 25cm (10in) square cake, mark the holes for the dowels using the blue dots inside the 20cm (8in) square, and if you are stacking a 15cm (6in) square cake onto a 20cm (8in) square cake, mark the holes for the dowels using the blue dots inside the 15cm (6in) square. Always also place one dowel right in the centre of each cake you are dowelling (on the green dot).

**2** Rub the rounded end of the dowels with a piece of sandpaper to remove any minor bumps, then remove the template and push one dowel into the cake at each mark, making sure that the dowels go in straight.

**3** Use an edible ink pen to mark each dowel at the level of the cake then remove all dowels, laying them side by side on a flat surface.

**4** Use the flat blade of a knife to make sure they are all level at the bottom end, and rotate all the dowels so that the pen marks are visible at the top. If your cake has been cut, filled and covered well, all the marks should be fairly level. However, it is very likely that with most cakes, the marks may vary by a millimetre or two. Choose the dowel with the highest mark then score all dowels to this length using a sharp knife.

**5** Snap the dowels along the scored mark and rub the cut ends with sandpaper to smooth. All dowels should now be the same length. Re-insert the dowels into the existing holes in the cake.

**6** Spread 15ml (1 tbsp) royal icing onto the centre of the cake and just covering all the dowels and position the smaller cake on top. This can be manipulated into position while the royal icing is still wet. Repeat steps 1–6 for any further tiers.

*Tip...*
*Leave your stacked cakes to settle for a couple of hours before trimming with ribbon, as the ribbon may wrinkle as your cakes settle slightly (see Trimming a Cake and Board with Ribbon in Techniques).*

# Piping and Flooding

You can create so many fantastic designs and effects simply by using a piping (pastry) bag and a tube (tip)! Kids love nothing better than trying to write their names in coloured icing, so let them loose with a filled bag and a piece of greaseproof (wax) paper and you'll be amazed at how quickly they master the techniques. Once they have the feel for it, it's easy to transfer their skills to a cake.

## Materials

- Royal icing
- Water
- Buttercream

## Equipment

- Piping (pastry) bags
- Piping tubes (tips)
- Small paintbrush
- Cocktail stick (toothpick)
- Basic equipment (see Basic Tools and Equipment)

## Piping with Royal Icing

**1** Snip the end of a piping (pastry) bag off at an angle, approx 1cm (⅜in) up from the tip. Slip in a tube (tip) (for most of the projects in this book we have used a no.2 tube/tip), then spoon in the royal icing.

**2** Twist the bag to force the icing towards the tip. Hold firmly in one hand, thumb over the top and fingers either side and steady with the other hand. Squeeze gently, holding the tube (tip) about 2cm (¾in) above the line you wish to pipe.

**3 To pipe dots** Touch the surface with the tube (tip) and gently squeeze until the dot is the required size, then release pressure and pull away. If the dot has a little peak, flatten it down by touching it gently with a damp paintbrush.

**4 To pipe outlines** Touch the tube (tip) down where you wish to begin and gently squeeze. As you squeeze, lift the tube (tip) slightly and follow the line you wish to pipe, allowing the icing to fall back down onto the surface. To finish piping, bring the tube (tip) back down to the surface and stop squeezing. When piping outlines, it is important to ensure there are no gaps in the outline or the flooding icing will leak out. Leave the outline to dry completely before flooding.

# Flooding with Royal Icing

**1** Thin out the royal icing with a few drops of water until it is the consistency of double cream. Add the water carefully, as a little goes a long way!

**2** Spoon the flooding icing into a piping (pastry) bag and snip off the very end. Fill in the outlines of the cookies by squeezing out some icing and using the cut end of the piping (pastry) bag or a cocktail stick (toothpick) to ease it into the corners. Take care not to squeeze out too much icing or it may overflow the outlines.

# Piping with Buttercream

**1** To pipe buttercream you will need large strong piping (pastry) bags and large tubes (tips). Otherwise, prepare, fill and pipe as you would with royal icing.

**2 To pipe swirls** Start piping from the outside edge of the cupcake and maintain a constant pressure, finishing with a peak in the centre of the cupcake.

**3 To pipe stars** Using a star tube (tip), hold the tip 2–3mm (1⁄16–1⁄8in) above the surface and squeeze gently. Once the star has formed, pull away sharply.

## Tip...

*Try mixing two colours of buttercream in the piping (pastry) bag to pipe swirls onto your cupcakes for a fun two-tone effect (see Psychedelic Cupcakes in Projects).*

# Figure Modelling

Don't be daunted by the idea of modelling figures such as the bears in the Teddy Bears' Picnic Cake (see Picnic Party in Projects) or the swans on the Winter Wonderland Cake (see White Christmas in Projects). The trick is to make each part of the figure separately (legs, arms, wings etc.) and assemble once dry.

## Materials
- Readymade sugardough or sugarpaste with the addition of CMC (Tylo) powder
- Edible glue or royal icing
- Dried spaghetti

## Equipment
- Cling film (plastic wrap)
- Drying mat
- Piping (pastry) bag and no.2 tube (tip)
- Foam or sponge offcuts
- Basic equipment (see Basic Tools and Equipment)

1 If using sugarpaste, add 5ml (1 tsp) CMC (Tylo) powder to every 200g (7oz) sugarpaste and incorporate well – this makes the sugarpaste firmer while remaining pliable and easy to work with. Whether using readymade sugardough or sugarpaste with CMC (Tylo) added, you will need to work quickly as the paste will dry out faster than usual. Tightly wrap any paste that is not being used immediately in cling film (plastic wrap).

2 Once you have modelled each section of the figure, set it aside to dry completely before assembling (unless instructed otherwise in a particular project), sticking the component parts together with dabs of edible glue or royal icing, and using sticks of dried spaghetti for extra strength where necessary.

### Tip...
*When making large figures such as teddy bears, it may be necessary to support some body parts with foam or sponge offcuts until the edible glue or royal icing has hardened.*

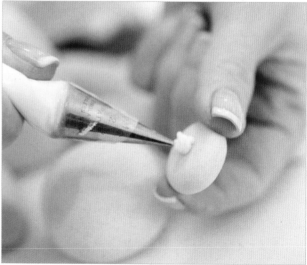

# Other Modelling Techniques

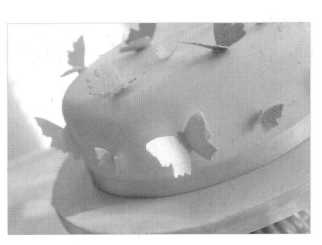

As well as modelling by hand, there are endless moulds and cutters available for cake decorating.

# Cutting Out Shapes

**1 For freehand cutting or cutting round a template** Use a very sharp craft knife to avoid wrinkling the paste and to give a clean edge.

**2 Using cutters** Position the cutter on top of the thinly rolled-out paste and press down firmly, twisting the cutter slightly. Remove the cut shape by tapping, or pushing gently in the centre with the rounded end of a paintbrush. Place on a foam mat to dry.

# Shaping Cut Outs

**1 Flowers** As soon as they have been cut out, place the flowers into a small cup shape (e.g. the well of a paint palette). Once dry, the flower will hold its shape. For small flowers, sugarpaste works well. For larger flowers, it is best to use thinly rolled petal paste, which hardens to a china-like consistency.

**2 Butterflies** Cut out the butterfly shape then dry each butterfly by resting it over a folded piece of card overnight.

*Tip...*
*Before pushing out your shapes, turn the cutter over and rub the palm of your hand over the edges of the cutter to ensure the shape comes out cleanly.*

# Display and Presentation

Half the fun of making special cakes or bakes, is seeing the reaction they provoke among friends and family. Displaying them in a fun and innovative way can make your creations seem even more amazing. There are many different ways to present your decorated cakes, cookies and treats and you are really only limited by your imagination. In this section, we have tried to give you some traditional ideas, alongside some quirky, more offbeat examples.

# Large Cakes

Set out beautifully on an iced board edged with ribbon, most cakes look stunning in their own right. However, to make your cake look even more special, place it on a beautiful glass or china stand on a pristine white tablecloth, scattered with brightly coloured confetti or ribbons in complementary colours. If you are making a three-tier cake, and don't have a stand to fit, then simply ice and ribbon two or three additional boards of increasing diameter in the same or complementary colours as the original board, and position your cake on these. If you are transporting your larger cakes to a different venue, plain boxes of all sizes are available from most sugarcraft shops and online suppliers.

# Cupcakes and Whoopie Pies

Depending on the occasion, cupcakes and whoopies can be presented in a variety of ways. There is a multitude of cupcake stands available on the market, from vintage china to ultra-modern Perspex – and even colourful disposable cardboard! Also, check out our special Halloween cupcake stand (see Happy Halloween in Projects). Of course cupcakes also look lovely displayed on plain white china or pretty plates, which can be found in most kitchens.

If everyone eats your cupcakes at your event – fantastic. However, if your cupcakes are to be used as take-home birthday favours or sold at bake sales, you need some way of getting them home in one piece. The days of a crumbling piece of cake in an old napkin at the bottom of a party bag are hopefully long gone! Now, the variety of boxes, domes, bags and other packaging ideas for cupcakes, which can be trimmed with ribbon and tagged for your guests to take home with them, is immense.

# Cookies

Many of our cookie projects look great displayed on simple white china, but if you are planning on selling a selection at a school fête, or giving them as a present, then there lots of different ways of packaging them. Many online and high-street stores sell cellophane bags – often decorated with brightly coloured pictures reflecting a particular occasion – Christmas, Halloween and so on – simply place one or more cookies into one of these bags, tie with coordinating curling ribbon and display on an attractive tray or in a pretty flowerpot or trug filled with colourful tissue paper.

If the cookies are for a present, why not really push the boat out? Display our Party Balloon Cookies (see Family Celebration in Projects) in a wicker basket lined with tissue paper and decorated with a floating helium balloon, or the Buzzy Bumblebee Cookies (see Picnic Party in Projects) on a colourful flower plate, or in a small tin pail lined with straw and hand tied with raffia, making a few flowers on wires to fly above the bees? Or finally, why not ice a board, and make it part of the story, like we did with our Blooming Bouquet Cookies (see Mother's Day Delights in Projects)? The possibilities are endless.

# Truffles

These little mouthfuls of gorgeousness can be arranged on a simple white plate, presented individually in petit four cakes inside tealight holders (perhaps as favours on a beautifully decorated Christmas table), or if you're feeling very decadent, piled in Martini glasses as a treat with coffee!

# Cake Pops and Lollipops

Cake pops exploded onto the baking scene recently, and there are now lots of packaging and display solutions available for these and for moulded lollipops. The simplest, and possibly most effective, is to place them in a clear cellophane bag, throw in a handful of colourful sprinkles and tie with a beautifully coloured ribbon. Cover a block of florists' oasis or a polystyrene cake dummy with colourful paper, and push the sticks firmly in – voila!

Alternatively, fill a pretty vase with sweets or coloured sugar and push the sticks in. You can also find boxes designed specifically for cake pops and lollipops – with readymade holes for the sticks, and cellophane windows. These can be decorated with stickers or tied with ribbon to make them special and personal.

# Other Ideas

There are so many everyday items that can be used to display and present your beautifully decorated cakes and cookies. Just the addition of a pretty satin ribbon tied around a board, or a bright piece of curling ribbon cascading from a cellophane bag filled with colourful cookies can elevate your creations to a higher level. Also, don't forget the humble doily – they are available in a variety of colours and shapes, and can be used to complement any arrangement.

Finally, always be on the lookout in second-hand shops and garden centres for quirky containers – small pails, boxes, plates, dishes, flowerpots and even delicate china cups and saucers – these can all be filled with treats, tied in cellophane, trimmed with curling ribbon and presented to friends and family for special occasions.

# Suppliers

## Great Britain

**Almond Art**
Units 15/16 Faraday Close,
Gorse Lane Industrial Estate, Clacton On Sea
Essex CO15 4TR
01255 223322
www.almondart.com
*Cake decorating, cake decorations
and sugarcraft supplies*

**FMM Sugarcraft**
Unit 5, Kings Park Industrial Estate,
Primrose Hill, Kings Langley
Hertfordshire WD4 8ST
01923 268699
www.fmmsugarcraft.com
*Sugarcraft manufacturers and suppliers
of cake decorating equipment*

**Knightsbridge PME Ltd**
Chadwell Heath Lane, Romford
Essex RN6 4NP
020 8590 5959
www.cakedecoration.co.uk
*UK distributor of Wilton products*

**Lakeland**
51 stores nationwide
01539 488100
www.lakeland.co.uk
*Kitchenware and general bakeware*

**Squires**
Squires Group, Squires House,
3 Waverley Lane, Farnham
Surrey GU9 8BB
0845 6171810
www.squires-shop.com
*Specialist bakeware, cake decorating
and sugarcraft supplies*

**Waitrose**
0800 188884
www.waitrose.com
*General baking ingredients and cake
decorating supplies*

## United States

**All In One Bake Shop**
8566 Research Blvd, Austin, TX 78758
512 371 3401
www.allinonebakeshop.com
*Cake making and decorating supplies*

**Global Sugar Art**
625 Route 3, Unit 3, Plattsburgh, NY 12901
800 420 6088
www.globalsugarart.com
*Everything sugarcraft*

**Wilton Industries, Inc.**
2240 West 75th Street, Woodridge, IL 60517
630 963 1818
www.wilton.com
*Innovative selection of baking and cake
decorating supplies*

## Australia

**Baking Pleasures**
PO Box 22, Corinda, QLD 4075
http://bakingpleasures.com.au/
*Baking and cake decorating products,
tools and equipment*

**Iced Affair**
53 Church Street, Camperdown, NSW 2050
02 9519 3679
www.icedaffair.com.au
*Specialist sugarcraft supplies*

**Planet Cake**
106 Beattie Street, Balmain, NSW 2041
02 9810 3843
www.planetcake.com.au
*Cake making and decorating supplies*

# About the Authors

Natalie Saville and Jill Collins co-own and run The Great Little Cake Company – a highly successful (and deliciously addictive) cake business, specializing in beautiful and creative wedding and celebration cakes. After the success of their first book, *Bake Me I'm Yours... Whoopie Pies* (D&C, 2011), Natalie and Jill decided to return to what inspired their business in the first place – decorating cakes with and for their children!

www.thegreatlittlecakecompany.co.uk

# Acknowledgments

We would like to thank everyone at D&C – particularly James, Charly and Grace – for their ongoing support and advice. Also, thanks once again to Ame for her brilliant editing and to Lorna for her amazing photographs, which really captured the essence of our cakes – and our children! Many thanks also to Julie, for allowing us to shoot most of the book in her truly beautiful kitchen, and of course, to the real stars of the show – our own gorgeous children – Ashley, Elena, Joe and Jake, and not forgetting the 'supporting cast' – Olivia, Lucy, Alexander, Nathaniel, James, Charlotte, Oscar and Eloise and their lovely mums – Helen, Alison, Julie, Lou and Keren.

# Templates

To download full-size printable PDFs of these templates go to

www.bakeme.com/templates

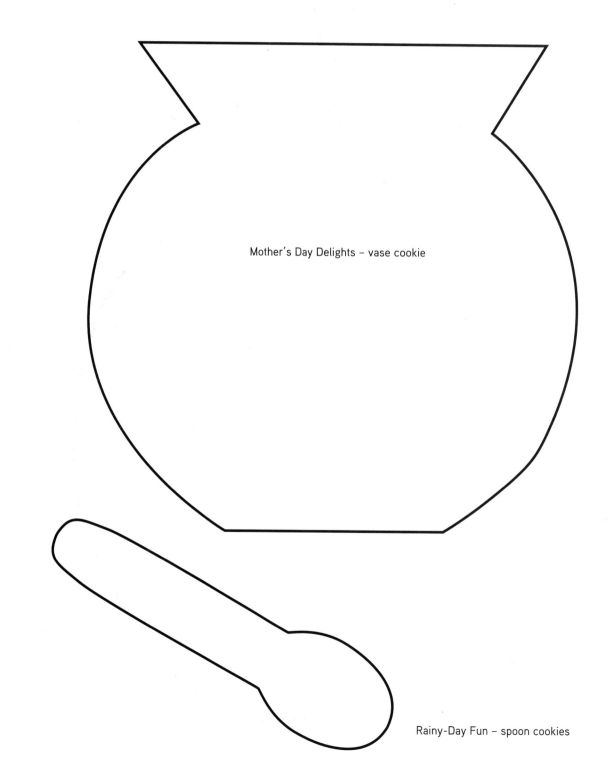

Mother's Day Delights – vase cookie

Rainy-Day Fun – spoon cookies

Dowelling template
(shown at half size)
enlarge by 200%

Yellow for round cakes
Blue for square cakes
Green for centre dowel

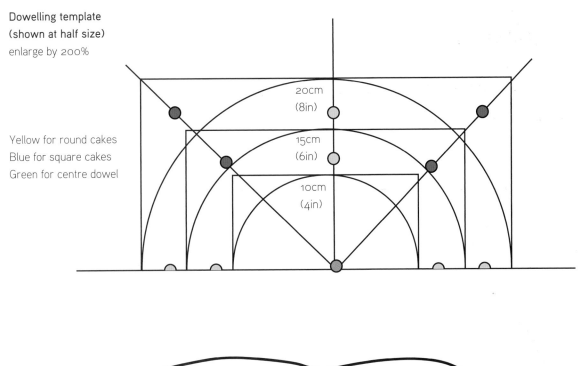

20cm
(8in)

15cm
(6in)

10cm
(4in)

Gifts for Teachers – apple cake
(shown at half size)
enlarge by 200% for a 30cm
(12in) round cake

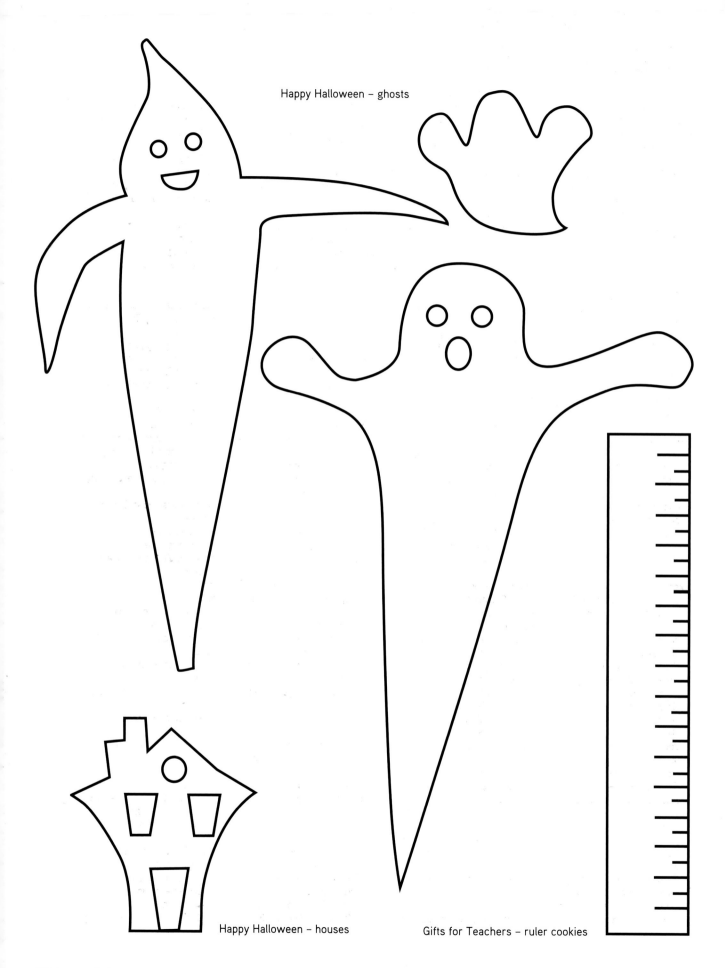

Happy Halloween – ghosts

Happy Halloween – houses

Gifts for Teachers – ruler cookies

# Index

## Dedication

To our gorgeous children – Ashley, Elena, Joe and Jake, who have helped us to make, decorate and eat countless fun and beautiful cakes over the last 13 years. Without them, and the numerous celebrations they have inspired, The Great Little Cake Company might never have been born.

A DAVID & CHARLES BOOK
© F&W Media International, Ltd 2012

David & Charles is an imprint of F&W Media International, Ltd
Brunel House, Forde Close, Newton Abbot, TQ12 4PU, UK

F&W Media International, Ltd is a subsidiary of F+W Media, Inc
10151 Carver Road, Cincinnati OH45242, USA

Text and Designs © Jill Collins & Natalie Saville 2012
Layout and Photography © F&W Media International, Ltd 2012

First published in the UK and USA in 2012

Jill Collins & Natalie Saville have asserted their right to be identified as authors of this work in accordance with the Copyright, Designs and Patents Act, 1988.

Names of manufacturers and product ranges are provided for the information of readers, with no intention to infringe copyright or trademarks.

A catalogue record for this book is available from the British Library.

ISBN-13: 978-1-4463-0212-5 paperback
ISBN-10: 1-4463-0212-1 paperback

Paperback edition printed in China by RR Donnelley for:
F&W Media International, Ltd
Brunel House, Forde Close, Newton Abbot, TQ12 4PU, UK

10 9 8 7 6 5 4 3 2 1

Acquisitions Editor: James Brooks
Assistant Editor: Grace Harvey
Project Editor: Ame Verso
Art Editor: Charly Bailey
Photographer: Lorna Yabsley
Senior Production Controller: Kelly Smith

F+W Media publishes high quality books on a wide range of subjects.
For more great book ideas visit: www.rucraft.co.uk